Partnerships in

Work Based Learning

Edited by

Veronica Swallow
Senior Lecturer
within the School of Health, Community and Education Studies
Northumbria University

Hazel Chalmers
Principal Lecturer
within the School of Health, Community and Education Studies
Northumbria University

John Miller
Associate Dean
Business and International Development
Northumbria University

northumbr˙
UNIVERSITY PRE

Published by Northumbria University Press
Trinity Building, Newcastle upon Tyne NE1 8ST, UK

First Published 2004

British Library Cataloguing in Publication Data. A Catalogue Record for this
book is available from the British Library.

ISBN 1–904794–03–3

Designed and printed by External Relations,
Northumbria University

Cover photography: Simon Veit-Wilson, with thanks to Sara McCafferty.

Northumbria University is the trading name of the University of Northumbria at Newcastle.
ER-93272-3/04

With grateful thanks to:

All the contributors who have patiently shared our journey to completion of the book and whose candid accounts of their own experiences have so richly illustrated the challenges and achievements the journey entailed; all the students and colleagues at Northumbria University and in local NHS Trusts who have been our 'partners in work based learning' over the last five years and whose experiences have helped to shape the book; Northumbria University Press, in particular Andrew Peden Smith and Jessica Clubbs for their expert guidance and support throughout the editorial process; Northern England Workforce Development Confederation who provided funding for the first Accredited Work Based Learning project which was subsequently a catalyst for the work described in the book.

CONTENTS

Preface

Professor Patrick Easen

School of Health, Community and Education Studies, Northumbria University

Although set in the context of health and social care, this book is an exploration of what constitutes effective professional education. In particular, it focuses on the challenges for Higher Education (HE), the workplace and the individual professional of the effective development of practice through Accredited Work Based Learning (AWBL). As Bennett points out in Chapter 6, the translation of learning into practice has remained an elusive goal of both professional educators and service managers. Work based learning, this book suggests, offers considerable potential for addressing the issue.

For the learner, it provides the missing 'fourth R' of education, 'relevance'. That, of course, does not make work based learning easy in any way. Piercy and Sen, in Chapter 4, and Gillson and Brooksbank, in Chapter 7, provide us with insights into the affective dimensions of participating in AWBL. Significant learning, we are reminded, is hard work and the journey through the 'cloud of unknowing' to new understandings of the supposedly familiar can be a source of considerable anxiety – a situation captured so brilliantly by Laing (1970) in his book of poems, *'Knots'*. Not surprisingly, then, although we may learn more about our professional activity, as Wimpenny in Chapter 8 points out, we also learn more about ourselves as people through the metacognition achieved by engagement in reflective processes.

For service managers, effective AWBL can deliver results. In the case study in Chapter 4, one measure of its success was in terms of appropriate patient referral by Emergency Nurse Practitioners (ENPs). Systematic study revealed that ENPs performed better than junior doctors. Other spin-offs, however, were an enhanced nursing workforce who felt empowered to challenge, in Foucault's (1972) phrase, the 'regimen of truth' in that context; thereby revealing the further potential available to the service.

So if AWBL has so much to offer the learners and the service, what does that imply for the University? It is here that AWBL presents the greatest challenge for it raises fundamental questions about the nature of professional knowledge. Situated cognition is the goal of AWBL, so, for example, rather than ignoring or denying the role of intuition in professional activity, as Chalmers, Swallow and Miller stress in Chapter 1, AWBL recognises, values and works with it. Learning, we are told by the same authors in Chapter 3, can be seen as a social process with language central to it. During AWBL not only is naming about 'meaning' but also, and this is what makes it so powerful, through renaming it enables 're-meaning'. As importantly, AWBL requires a reconceptualisation of that overused HE word, 'employability'. Rather than being an outcome (amongst many) of HE learning, employability becomes the defining concept for the design, delivery and assessment of HE learning. On the way a number of shibboleths of learning in HE are destroyed. In Chapters 9 and 10, for example, the authors illustrate how the traditional Masters dissertation, something that might be cynically described as a vehicle for reinforcing the power relationship between academic and student, transforms to become the Practice Project. Thus it becomes a tool for engaging not only with the norms of practice in the workplace but also with the professional cultures that give meaning to those norms and the power relations that sustain them.

This book, offers practitioners, service managers, professional educators and policy makers both a vision of how practice in the workplace may be developed and some very useful advice on how that might be achieved. Organisational change may be glacial but, the authors suggest, AWBL may become the educational equivalent of global warming for both the workplace and the University.

Background and Introduction

Veronica Swallow, Hazel Chalmers and John Miller

As an academic framework based in practice, Accredited Work Based Learning (AWBL) enables practitioners to identify their own work based learning needs, develop individual outcomes relating to their developing practice, supports them as they achieve the outcomes and assists them to critically reflect upon their on-going learning. During this process they are also able to meet service delivery and organisational needs (Swallow, Chalmers & Miller, 2001).

This book emerged from our combined experiences of responding to requests from National Health Service (NHS) Trusts to develop flexible education that meets the needs of a modern and continuously changing health care workforce. There is a growing interest in the day-to-day learning that occurs at work as practitioners strive to give high quality care to patients, with limited resources. This is against a background of growing expectations that the same practitioners will continuously refine and develop their practice and be 'lifelong learners'. Long-standing professional boundaries are being challenged and new and more diverse roles are emerging, yet education appears not to have kept pace with these changes (Chalmers & Bond, 1997). Therefore, NHS Trusts are increasingly looking for cost-effective, flexible means of educating the workforce quickly and efficiently (Ayer & Smith, 1998) and there is a growing professional requirement for staff to demonstrate continuing professional development (UKCC, 1992).

A recent review of workforce planning in the NHS recommends flexible working to make best use of the range of skills and knowledge which staff possess, the development of new and more flexible careers for staff and the modernisation of education and training (DoH, 2000) to ensure staff are equipped to work in a complex and often turbulent service. In response to these combined factors, we embarked on the fascinating journey to develop an academic framework, based in practice which could allow practitioners' on-going learning to be acknowledged and valued in a way that was not, at that time, possible with conventional educational approaches.

The History of Accredited Work Based Learning

Several of the authors underwent a series of learning and developmental experiences with accreditation before arriving at the examples of AWBL reported in this book. Although AWBL is now accepted as an innovative, flexible and customer responsive learning methodology, early examples of accreditation were often of prior learning, e.g. Accreditation of Prior Learning (APL). This approach has its origins in the early 1990s when most Higher Education Institutions (HEIs) were ensuring their programmes of study were in keeping with the Credit Accumulation and Transfer Scheme (CATS) philosophy of the time. With CATS Higher Education (HE) was required to move towards unitisation or modularisation in curriculum design to allow movement between programmes and in some instances between institutions.

In the early 1990s, new curricula at diploma and degree level were in some respects experimenting with units or modules of study. The terms unitisation and modularisation have been used interchangeably for several years, while the contemporary terminology and language favours modules and modularisation. However, the concept of structuring learning in this way is the same. At Newcastle Polytechnic, now Northumbria University, a Diploma in Nursing Studies programme was developed offering 60 credits at Level Two[1], while the remaining 60 credits would be achieved through previous or past 'assessed' learning. Unfortunately, although Nursing Colleges, at that time outside of HEIs, were also seeking academic accreditation for their programmes of study, there were not sufficient nurses already holding academic credit to apply for the 60 credit Diploma in Nursing Studies programme.

This 'over' expectation on the qualified nursing market resulted in the need to develop alternative ways to gain academic credit. Accreditation of Prior Experiential Learning (APEL) appeared to emerge as the favoured strategy for students to gain recognition and subsequently gain advanced standing through programmes. Early developments at Newcastle Polytechnic were influenced by other successful schemes around the country; one being at Sheffield Hallam Polytechnic, who offered students academic recognition for portfolios of evidence measured against unit learning outcomes.

Most APEL schemes emphasised the need to develop themes and write learning outcomes. Being a retrospective methodology, most qualified nurses had considerable experience to relate to. Unfortunately for both the student and the teacher, portfolios of evidence were excessive to the point of being carried in large carrier bags. Although very interesting, most APEL portfolios were rooted in the past and didn't give an indication of any new knowledge or current learning the student was now engaged in. Reflection was a key element to considering past experience and critical incidents were often used as evidence. However, as one nurse reported, APEL did not allow them to interact with their current practice, to question decisions they had made or to resolve those difficult day-to-day problems encountered in nursing. In many respects APEL's days were numbered for us on the occasion when four supermarket carrier bags, accompanied by a stressed nurse, were submitted as a portfolio of evidence in an APEL exercise!

In some respects AWBL came in the format discussed in this book out of necessity. The demands of contemporary health care, and in particular the National Health Service (NHS) Trusts, required new ways of working. Demands of the service meant little time for attending University to undertake taught programmes of study. New practitioner roles demand current and ongoing learning, more so than APL or APEL could ever offer because of their retrospective nature. AWBL has been seen as rewarding learning that is relevant to practice now and can be used within or towards further academic study.

Moreover, it can be argued that AWBL has created interdependence between theory and practice. It would appear logical that as a consequence of writing about and questioning current practice a theoretical base is used to generate arguments. However, questioning and challenging current practice will inevitably rock the foundations of such a theoretical base. This process of challenge illustrates the Personal Constructed Theory of Learning purported by Claxton (1984). In itself this can be threatening to the leaner but can also be a means of revealing new knowledge. It could be argued that APL and APEL were created as mechanisms to enhance the workings of a CATS conceived at the birth of unitisation. As tools of efficiency APL and APEL may have limited currency in the improvement and development of practice, which leaves us to reflect on the possible benefits of AWBL, it:

- Is current
- It encourages reflection on and in practice
- It challenges existing theory
- It generates new ideas and as an added bonus it allows the student to gain recognition through academic credit.

Developing the AWBL framework

When, in 1998, we began searching for material to inform the development of AWBL we found that existing literature in health care tended to focus on course based educational developments or practice developments rather than on an integrated approach to practice and education in health care. The notion of giving credit for health care practitioners' learning at work was not new, but we could find no examples of an integrated approach which was flexible enough to respond to the needs of a rapidly changing health service and rigorous enough to meet the quality standards of HE and NHS Trusts.

Around the time that the AWBL development began at Northumbria University a new body of emerging literature began to appear relating to workplace learning from a generic perspective (Garrick, 1998; Boud & Garrick, 1999; Boud & Solomon, 2001). This highlights the fact that the world of work is changing radically and that the concepts of 'work' and 'learning' are no longer separate entities. The terms 'knowledge worker' and 'learning organisation' are becoming widespread and,

> *'... this development is accompanied by a shift away from viewing educational institutions as the principal places of "valid" learning towards recognition of the power and importance of workplaces as sites of learning. Enterprises need integrated approaches to change. New notions of learning at work offer exciting ways of achieving this by challenging boundaries within and between organisations and exploring new ways of being at work.'*
> (Boud & Garrick, 1999, p.3)

Boud and Garrick (2001) have started to move forward the discussion to try and understand learning at work from this generic perspective. They recognise the multi-faceted nature of workplace learning and conclude that there can be no universal model for learning at work. It was, therefore, the dearth of documented evidence in relation to the idea of valuing work based learning in health care education, in particular for nurses, that was the catalyst for this book.

In health care there has been a positive move towards promoting and valuing HE/Clinical partnerships which create an educational climate that enables nurses to engage in theoretical analysis and practice to increase personal and professional growth (Birchenall, 1999). According to Waddington and Marsh (1999), shared responsibility for planning and creating the learning process is a key feature of experiential learning, and other authors emphasise the benefits of collaboration in workplace learning (Winter & Maisch, 1996; Jarvis, 1999; Chalmers *et al.* 2001). The benefits of taking the learning to the learners in their own setting and building upon what they already know has been highlighted by

Lueddeke (1997) as invaluable for those who have traditionally been denied access to advanced standing for HE because of personal, socio-economic or institutional constraints.

It is our intention, therefore, to try to begin to address the shortfall in the information available to us during the process of developing AWBL by producing a comprehensive book which explores some of the challenges we, our colleagues and our students encountered when developing and delivering the AWBL framework. A key feature of the book is that it is written by and for health care professionals who work and learn at the interface between service and higher education. The editors decided to present the developments that occurred between 1998 and 2002 from as broad a range of perspectives as possible.

This is why there are contributions from service providers who had commissioned AWBL projects and from experienced practitioners who have undertaken study on project based and programme based AWBL. In addition there are contributions from other educationalists within Northumbria University who had taken a similar approach and adapted it to meet the needs of different cohorts of students in different work settings.

The range of AWBL activity in the University is wider than that which is presented here. In the book, however, we have tried to capture the essence of the learning about AWBL that has occurred for us during the development. In addition, we aim to articulate it in what we hope will be a meaningful way for colleagues who may consider adopting this approach in their own institutions. This is not intended as a guide book on how to 'do' AWBL, rather an introduction to a particular philosophical approach to work based learning which has, we believe, covered new ground in relation to collaborative working between HE and the NHS. By presenting this broad range of experiences we hope the reader will be able to make a well informed judgement about the value of this educational approach and its potential for the future.

The design and structure of the book

The book has been designed to introduce the reader to educational theories underpinning the AWBL approach, with particular reference to the shift towards competence based learning; to explore and discuss the case for recognising and rewarding learning at work from the HE and service perspective and to illustrate the experiences of practitioners who participated in the process leading to accreditation of their work based learning. With this in mind the book is written in three parts.

Part 1 takes a theoretical and analytical approach to these issues and includes contributions from Senior Trust based colleagues as well as Senior Educationalists, all of whom have experience of working on different AWBL developments over the last four years.

In Chapter 1, the editors set the scene using earlier research (Chalmers & Bond, 1997) which found that even though new nursing roles involved higher levels of decision-making and different skills, there was no academic or professional recognition via assessment and accreditation. In addition, there was no synergy between nurses' development needs and service development needs, and existing educational provision was not wholly appropriate for these new roles. Educational theories underpinning AWBL are explored and discussed. These include the Cognitive Apprenticeship Model, Scaffolding and the concept of the Zone of Proximal Development. The authors suggest that as health care changes, educationalists ought to engage in more risk taking strategies involving teaching and learning approaches which can act as catalysts for lifelong learning. Finally, it is argued that collaboration with stakeholders is both theoretically and practically essential for successful outcomes to the AWBL process.

Chapter 2, takes the form of a transcribed conversation between Professor Mary Dunning and Hazel Chalmers who explore the way in which educational imperatives are placed in context with the prevailing policy environment surrounding HE and health care. Professor Dunning argues that if AWBL is to become more mainstream in HE it needs to be given the same level of credence as any traditional provision, in the same way that Northumbria University is beginning to do – that it needs to be open to critical scrutiny from peers as well as subjected to being researched and evaluated, and finally that it is supported by appropriately skilled people.

In Chapter 3, John Miller, Hazel Chalmers and Veronica Swallow discuss the first AWBL project they developed between Northumbria University and Newcastle upon Tyne Hospitals NHS Trust. Using this as an example they illustrate the way in which collaborative consultation was used in 'customising' education for a group of nurses undergoing significant role development at a time of major service development. The value and significance of such a collaborative approach is seen as both collegial and egalitarian and formed the basis for many further customised AWBL developments.

Taking the theme of collaboration a step further in Chapter 4, Chris Piercy, a key clinical stakeholder in the first AWBL project, describes the journey from identification of a major training need for two experienced Accident and Emergency nurses to completion of the project. He explains how this method of preparing staff and influencing clinical practice has now become embedded in other developments across the Trust. He lists the benefits as: improved, mutual understanding between service and HE, a reduction in the education/practice gap, opportunities to work collaboratively on research and practice development projects and to disseminate aspects of these collaborative venture.

In Chapter 5, John Unsworth poses the question, 'Does AWBL have a role in developing Primary Health Care Staff?' In exploring this question John uses three case studies as examples of AWBL developments in Primary Care. These were a response to service development needs while also providing opportunities for Continuing Professional Development (CPD) of staff, including staff in a local Leisure Centre. While acknowledging certain limitations of the customised AWBL process, he concludes that the AWBL approach does very effectively allow universities to respond to service needs at a time of unprecedented change.

In Chapter 6, Joanne Bennett describes how she and a colleague used the AWBL Framework in a Primary Care Trust to develop an AWBL programme for community nurses. The overall aim was to support front-line practitioners to develop knowledge and competencies commensurate with their changing role. As providers of education, she argues, that we have a responsibility to work in partnership with service colleagues to provide flexible education which prepares practitioners for their changing role in practice.

Part 2 focuses on the practitioner experience of work based learning at diploma, degree and Masters levels and demonstrates the wide range of learning opportunities that exist in the practice setting and the way in which practitioners' creativity can be harnessed and converted into academic credit.

The experience of being students on the first two AWBL cohorts in Newcastle Hospitals NHS Trust, is reflected upon with candour by Julie Gillson and Mathew Brooksbank in Chapter 7. This project based AWBL presented them with a maelstrom of difficulties and successes but led eventually to them both achieving success in clinical role development and academic recognition at Level 3. They describe how they have used their increased confidence acquired during the educational experience to become reflexive and autonomous practitioners working in new and innovative roles.

The student experience of programme based AWBL and its impact on her evolving role as a Sister and educationalist in Critical Care is critically analysed by Sarah Wimpenny in Chapter 8. The AWBL experience gave Sarah the opportunity to explore how her own personal and professional development had evolved since her career began in the Intensive Care Unit (ITU), back in 1993. She was able to examine how previous professional development had influenced her in taking steps to bridge the theory practice gap in her workplace.

In Chapter 9, John Miller, Margaret Best and Jill Robson discuss how they worked within a tripartite contract of learning to support Jill, a Senior Sister in a District General Hospital, as she introduced Patient Focused Care (PFC) into the Trust within the framework of the MA Advanced Practice at Northumbria University. Having set out to discuss the work based learning that arose within a tripartite contract, it become evident that Jill was not the only 'learner'. The benefit of Jill, Margaret and John's collaboration meant that each could make their own contribution while also benefiting from the others' knowledge and experience.

Chapter 10 looks at an example of accredited work based learning at Masters level as Maggie Coates and Andrew Mellon compare their experiences as student and clinical mentor in developing an aspect of Paediatric Practice while Maggie undertook the MA Advanced Practice. Reflecting on the learning that occurred, Maggie, an experienced Senior Children's Nurse and Andrew, an experienced Consultant Paediatrician believe that the learning process and the professional working relationship established between two health professionals from different professional backgrounds during this educational experience will have longstanding benefits for patient care and mutual professional understanding.

Finally, in Part 3 the editors summarise the main perspectives of the book and synthesise the learning that has occurred during the journey. Using a triangulated approach, involving reflection within a metacognitive model, experience and research, they conclude that the journey has been one of 'learning about the learning' for all involved, and has led to creation of the Collaborative, Dynamic Practitioner Development (CDPD) Model (p. 175). This model is both flexible and adaptable while having the potential to be transferred to other settings and contexts at the interface between Higher Education and health care.

The book, therefore, reflects the synergy that can exist between clinical practice and education and we anticipate that it will have relevance throughout the UK as well as overseas, and be valuable to health care professionals (whether they are managers, past, present or potential students), teaching staff, health care researchers and workforce planners.

Note

[1] Academic levels now comply with the QAA Qualifications Framework and what was previously Level 2 is now Level 5.

References

Ayer, S. and Smith, C. (1998) 'Planning flexible learning to match the needs of consumers: a national survey.' *Journal of Advanced Nursing* (27) pp. 1,034–1,047.

Birchenall, P. (1999) 'Developing a work based learning philosophy.' *Nurse Education Today* (19) pp. 173–174.

Boud, D. and Garrick, J. (1999) *Understanding learning at work.* (Routledge, London).

Boud, D., Solomon, N. and Symes, C. (2001) *New practices for new times in work-based learning – a new Higher Education?* (Open University Press, Bucks).

Chalmers, H. and Bond, S. (1997) *Educational requirements for new nursing roles. Research report.* (Northumbria University & Centre for Health Services Research, University of Newcastle upon Tyne).

Chalmers, H., Swallow, V. and Miller, J. (2001) 'Accredited Work Based Learning: an approach for collaboration between Higher Education and practice.' *Nurse Education Today* (21) pp. 587–606.

Department of Health (2000) *A health service of all the talents: developing the NHS workforce.* Consultation document on the Review of Workforce Planning. (DoH, London).

Garrick, J. (1998) *Informal Learning in the Workplace: Unmasking Human Resource Development* (Routledge, London).

Jarvis, P. (1999) 'The Practitioner Researcher: developing theory from practice.' *Nurse Education Today* (20) pp. 30–35.

Lueddeke, G. (1997) 'The Accreditation of Prior Experiential Learning in Higher Education: a discourse on rationales and assumptions.' *Higher Education Quarterly* 51(3) pp. 210–24.

Smith, L. (1991) *Experiential learning* in Pendleton, S. and Myles, A. (eds) *Curriculum Planning in Nurse Education* (Edward Arnold, London).

Swallow, V., Chalmers, H. and Miller, J. (2000a) 'Learning on the job: accredited Work Based Learning (AWBL).' *Emergency Nurse* (8) 6 (October) pp. 35–39.

Swallow, V., Chalmers, H. and Miller, J. (2000b) 'Evaluating the development of Accredited Work Based Learning (AWBL) scheme for A&E nurses.' *Emergency Nurse* 8 (7) pp. 33–39.

Swallow, V., Chalmers, H., Miller, J., Piercy, C. and Sen, B. (2001) 'Accredited Work Based Learning (AWBL): Nurses' experiences of two pilot schemes.' *Journal of Clinical Nursing – Research in Brief* (10) pp. 820–821.

United Kingdom Central Council for Nursing, Midwifery and Health Visiting (1992) *The scope of professional practice.* (UKCC, London).

Waddington, K. and Marsh, L. (1999) 'Work based learning: implications for team and practice development.' *Advancing Clinical Nursing* (3) pp. 33–36.

Winter, R. and Maisch, M. (1996) *Professional Competence and Higher Education: The ASSET Programme* (The Falmer Press, London).

Part I

The case for Accredited Work Based Learning

Chapter 1

The theoretical perspective of Accredited Work Based Learning

Hazel Chalmers, Veronica Swallow and John Miller

In this chapter we explore the shift which is taking place within Higher Education (HE) in recognising the value of work based learning. Some of the educational theories that underpin Accredited Work Based Learning (AWBL) lead the discussion to the conclusion that collaboration with stakeholders is, both theoretically and practically, a categorical must.

Introduction

It is an indisputable fact that HE must make every attempt to align its provision with the political, technical and educational contexts within which it exists. At the same time quality assurance and enhancement cannot be compromised. Continuing Professional Development (CPD) is high on the agenda of the National Health Service (NHS) as a means of achieving government targets for health, but also for job satisfaction and retention of staff.

There are new ways of providing education involving closer collaboration with commissioners to ensure relevance. The teaching role is changing, appropriately, from that of 'expert academic', often using a didactic, information giving approach to 'facilitative academic', who enters into a 'partnership' with learners. In the latter approach, the 'threat' of learning is acknowledged and the learner and teacher enter into a mutually beneficial partnership. The teacher takes account of the pressures that impact on the learner, helping them to engage in the learning process and to cope with changing work environments.

Changing working roles generate CPD needs which are often addressed 'on the job'. Teachers can take greater account of and value the learners' previous knowledge and experience and can capitalise on this as a basis for further learning and development, thus facilitating ownership of and engagement in lifelong learning.

Educational theories used to underpin work based learning
The increasing emphasis on professional development

In *Working Together – Learning Together* (2001), Alan Milburn acknowledges the link between lifelong learning and success in the NHS:

> *'Learning and development are key to delivering the Government's vision of patient centred care in the NHS. Lifelong learning is about growth and opportunity, about making sure that our staff, the teams and organisations they relate to, and work in, can acquire new knowledge and skill, both to realise their potential and to help shape and change things for the better.'*

Thus the need for synergy between practice, service delivery and ongoing professional development is clearly recognised. However, while there is general agreement that ongoing learning and development is intrinsically 'good', it could also be argued that there is presently little or no coherence as to how or to what standard this can be achieved. Chalmers and Bond (1997) found that on-the-job learning was being undertaken by nurses who were adopting new nursing roles. Moreover, even though the roles involved higher levels of decision-making and different skills, there was no academic or professional recognition via accreditation and assessment. Nor was there explicit synergy between the nurses' development and service needs. In addition, existing university based programmes within the NHS contract for CPD was not wholly appropriate for changing nurses' roles.

Eraut (1994) comments that Initial Professional Education (IPE) attempts to provide all the knowledge required for a 'lifetime in the profession', and that there is little, if any, link to ongoing learning. He differentiates between Continuing Professional Education (CPE) as off-the-job learning and CPD which he suggests is a combination of formally organised education *and* work based learning. Whilst there may be a professional requirement to attend CPE, he asserts, there is rarely any requirement to demonstrate continuing competence to practice. The Department of Health (July 1999), however, interprets CPD as,

> *'... focused on the needs of patients and should help individuals and teams deliver the health outcomes and health care priorities of the NHS, as set out in national service frameworks and local health improvement programmes.'*

This is clearly a means to achieving local and national targets as well as personal and professional (learning) needs. The DoH (*ibid.*) cites the accreditation of organisations as 'Investors in People' as one approach to CPD but the document goes on to state that '*work based learning will play an increasingly important part in CPD*'. The way forward it would seem is to design education for CPD which combines the needs of all stakeholders including patients; a not inconsiderable task. Anecdotal evidence, derived from midwifery, suggests that practitioners' and managers' views of educational needs differ. Given that; Higher Education Institutions (HEIs) have student targets to meet, the NHS must take into account national drivers; different stakeholders have different agendas, the issues involved in reconciling these differences in education is complex.

It is widely recognised that the health and social care arena is rapidly changing (UKCC, 1999; Birchenall, 2000) and the momentum of these changes is compelling practitioners to review their skill and knowledge base. Frequently, however, education fails to respond quickly enough and traditional provision may not include the broadening knowledge and skill base recommended by Birchenall (*ibid.*). Educationalists must shed the 'time warp' of traditional educational convention and engage in more risk taking strategies that involve a radical change to those teaching and learning approaches which act as catalysts for lifelong learning.

Education for professional competence

One such approach is evident in the Accreditation and Support for Specified Expertise and Training (ASSET) programme implemented by Anglia Polytechnic University and Essex Social Services Department (Winter & Maisch, 1996). This clearly demonstrated that a work based competence model of education can be used in initial preparation of social work and engineering students. Their belief that '*professional knowledge develops through the accumulation of concrete experience*' was confirmed through comparing their approach to other learning formats. The indications were that the competence based curriculum evaluated most positively overall, especially in relation to relevance to work and level of interest/motivation.

The post-Dearing emphasis on employability, relevance to work, lifelong learning and maintaining practitioner competence has, to some extent, allayed the early suspicions aroused by the Governments' National Vocational Qualification (NVQ) initiatives. The approach of making explicit the skill and the underpinning knowledge base used in NVQs has partially ameliorated the sceptical elitist view associated with academia held by many in higher education. Higher education institution's perceptions of competence must now include the '*dynamic concept of capability, embracing learning, culture and values*' (O'Reilly *et al.* 1999, p. 3), not merely the ability to perform a skill.

Thus the view of competence has evolved from the notion of the characteristics which enable a person to do a job well to include the aptitude and knowledge to perform well and consistently. Difficulty in defining competence has been highlighted by Eraut (1998), however, the integration of capability and performance, he claims, results in,

> *'... a critical approach to practice and a flexible mind, which enable a person to adapt and change and to become a proponent of change and creator of new professional knowledge.'*

Competence, he argues will change in different contexts and with different jobs. So that a competent person will have the ability to adapt and develop their knowledge and skill base and thus change their capability and performance. This is an essential element of competence focused work based learning.

Models of professional learning

Many models of professional learning have evolved to represent a continuum from apprenticeship to the reflective practitioner. According to Atkinson and Claxton (2000, p. 2) models vary in their relationship with *'reasoned performance'*. They report that it is the combination of conscious articulation of knowledge with intuitive ways of knowing which may be what 'works best'. Taking the continuum into account it is clear that a single model will not 'work best' for all learners. Practitioners with post-registration/qualified experience, often working as 'experts' in their field, differ in their approaches to learning from those of students in their initial preparation course.

The cognitive apprenticeship model relies on the expertise of an experienced practitioner facilitating the learners' development by socialisation into 'communal enterprise'. This approach is seen by some as little more than the 'sitting by Nellie' model used in many professional programmes two or more decades ago. However, the success of this model is not only the introduction of a novice to a culture as described by Lave and Wenger (1991), it also relies upon the expert making explicit the strategies by which the novice can develop competence (Cope *et al.* 2000).

Because many professionals engaged in work based learning are experienced practitioners, they are already members of the culture and have developed their own strategies to manage uncertainty and new situations. They may however, be novices in making explicit the implicit knowledge they use daily and the sources of that knowledge. These learners already have personal constructs of professional practice derived from their social context and culture. Their learning is best focused on questioning those constructs and engaging with the change process. This involves accepting that there is more than one 'right' answer, dealing with uncertainty and the capacity to use existing competence in unfamiliar contexts by extending and adapting existing skills.

Intuition in professional practice and development

Many practitioners are able to 'read' the situations in which they find themselves and use what Eraut (1994) refers to as situational knowledge. Knowledge which, according to Easen and Wilcockson (1996) enables an 'expert' to function intuitively, that is use an *'irrational process* (in decision-making) *that has a rational basis.'*

The place of intuition in professional decision-making is widely acknowledged (Easen & Wilcockson *ibid.*; Atkinson & Claxton 2000; Harbison, 2001; McCutcheon & Pincombe, 2001). Most authors base their arguments on the seminal work of Schon (1987) whose interpretation is *'reflection in action'*. Whilst there may not be total agreement on the nature of intuition, there is very strong agreement that it is a fundamental element of professional decision-making, can be validated, is speedy and uses a relevant knowledge base (Easen & Wilcockson *op. cit.*). The relevant knowledge base includes empirical, professional and technical sources and ways of thinking.

Work based learning capitalises on and attempts to capture the source of intuition, making explicit the sources of knowledge which inform intuitive practice and developing the competence base of the learner. Thus whilst the use of intuition may be thought of as unsound because the knowledge base is implicit, it allows for a constructionist view of reality, that is the use of 'artistry' rather than the technical rationality view which relies on facts and testable beliefs (Schon *op. cit.*). Intuition is anything but 'gut reaction,' it is deeply internalised knowledge and experience.

Therefore, the technical-rational model of decision-making constrains the practitioner rather than freeing him/her to be creative and innovative in finding solutions. Thus, as the practitioner becomes more skilled and experienced they become more reflective, both on and in practice. Reflection leads to the identification and use of other sources of knowledge to provide a bigger picture, resulting in the development of principles of professional practice and the cognitive skills of critical judgement.

Reflection in the workplace

Through reflection practitioners are able to recognise and articulate 'incidental' as well as explicit learning that occurs in their daily work (McGivney, 1999). Reflection is, therefore, increasingly regarded as a vehicle for learning (Schon, 1987; Boud & Walker, 1991; Smith, 1998; Cowan, 1998) and this is one of the central principles of the AWBL approach. In AWBL the challenge for the educationalist, as facilitator of the student's learning, is to guide the student away from the more traditional notion of classroom based learning to one which recognises and values the learning opportunities that are present in the workplace and help them to capitalise upon these opportunities. This shift of attitude can be quite stressful for the student who is accustomed to 'compartmentalising' their busy working life so that work is about 'doing the job' while learning has to be regarded as secondary and peripheral to work (Perry, 2000; Swallow, Chalmers & Miller, 2000).

Practitioners who enter the AWBL process can often demonstrate evidence of having undertaken vast amounts of learning to support their ongoing role development but then find that this carries little or no academic recognition. Moreover, although this learning is often initiated and supported by the student's employer, where this is not possible, perhaps for financial or logistical reasons, then it may be initiated by the practitioner themselves, sometimes self-funded and/or completed in their own time (Birchenall, 1999; Swallow, Chalmers & Miller, 2000; Chalmers, Swallow & Miller, 2001; Swallow, *et al.* 2001). Practitioners' attitudes to learning are, of course, determined to some extent by the prevailing learning culture of the workplace and there is increasing debate around the issues of informal and non-formal learning at work; the emphasis appears to be on the value of the processes and experiences involved as well as the context within which the learning occurs.

> *'Informal learning should no longer be regarded as an inferior form of learning whose main purpose is to act as the precursor of formal learning; it needs to be seen as fundamental, necessary and valuable in its own right.'*
> (Coffield, 2000).

Eraut (2000) promotes three typologies of non-formal learning:

- Implicit learning – the acquisition of knowledge independently of conscious attempts to learn and without explicit knowledge about what was learned.
- Reactive learning – explicit learning that takes place spontaneously and in response to current situations but without time set aside for it.
- Deliberative learning – planned learning with time set aside for the explicit learning process.

However, concern has been expressed in the literature on reflection that some nursing knowledge which is rooted in a medical model is in danger of being lost because of the fact that nurses often engage emotionally with their work. In addition, Smith (1998) suggests that nurses may believe this informal (or implicit) learning to be unworthy of recognition by themselves or articulation to their colleagues. In the AWBL process it is vital that a work based seminar/workshop approach supported by on-going tutorials, all facilitated by an educationalist, is used to introduce students to the main concepts and processes involved. This *deliberative* learning includes reflective practice, development of personal learning outcomes, negotiation of a learning contract and creation of a portfolio of evidence.

By nurturing a reflective approach during these sessions the students are supported to reflect upon the *reactive* learning that has occurred for them during their daily work, and to begin to conceptualise it in the light of relevant theory. In this way students can begin to recognise the informal work based learning that has taken place for them, often incidentally. They can then be guided to articulate this learning within a reflective account and a portfolio of evidence, thus developing their insight into their own learning. The role of the educationalist is to act as a facilitator. According to Rogers (1983), the teacher ought to enable learning by being a fellow explorer with the student. In this way learning will be based upon the student's own knowledge (Knowles, 1984) and the way in which they use that knowledge in the conduct of their work (Liaschenko & Fisher, 1999). In addition, Earnshaw (1995) and Spouse (1998) recommend that students should be encouraged to select a work based mentor who knows them and their particular learning style so that they are able to identify learning opportunities and optimise learning at work (Swallow & Coates, 2004). Thus work based seminars/tutorials/workshops become a forum for frank and open discussion between students and the facilitator where students can compare experiences of achieving learning outcomes while developing their academic skills.

According to Cook and Pickard (1997) assessment is a major motivator, and the significance of assessments as a means of learning should not be underestimated. Day *et al.* (1998) claim that the methods used to assess students are amongst the most critical of all influences on their learning. Indeed students often emerge from the work based learning assessment process able to demonstrate metacognitive skills (Fonteyn & Cahill, 1998) and an ability to be reflexive in practice as well as reflective (Swallow & Coates, 2004). However, the learning journey through work based learning and reflection is not without some potential hazards.

The 'threat' of learning

O'Rielly (1999) summarises a reflective conversation between Schon and eminent educationalists on the subject of professional capability. Reflection, Schon propounds, can be threatening, for it may involve examination of personal emotions and behaviour resulting in feelings of threat and defensiveness (p. 13). Claxton (1984) identifies four beliefs that create threat and impede learning. These beliefs, tied up with feelings of personal worth, identity, sanity and equilibrium, are that, as a human being, a person needs to feel *'competent, consistent, in control and comfortable'*. Unless these beliefs are challenged, according to Claxton, a person is unable to change their personal view of the world and therefore cannot learn. These 'four Cs' when activated reduce the capacity to tolerate *'strangeness'* and increase the frequency to *'resort to escape, defence and demolition.'* The process of reflection can raise issues the learner finds difficult and has the potential to impede learning and personal growth. The role of the teacher and the nature of the learning environment therefore become fundamentally important in realising growth and development.

The complexity of the professional and cultural situation in the work setting can enhance or impede professional learning. As Cope *et al.* (2000) point out *'acceptance into the community of practice is important'*. Acceptance is also determined by the *'working relationships within and between organisations'* (Barr, 1998). The drive towards inter-professional practice can raise feelings of threat and exacerbate professional boundaries and cultures. Cultures that have evolved from different knowledge bases, beliefs and values. Add to this the Government's drive to include service users and external representatives in organisational decisions plus the divisions in health care of private, public and voluntary sectors and it can be seen that there will be many layers of culture each with its own agenda. Often this agenda includes preservation of the status quo. Dealing with these multiple layers must, therefore, be managed with care where there are learners in the practice situation. For it is the learners who are at the interface and who learn to juggle the demands and counter demands. When the practice setting also becomes the learning environment additional tensions can arise.

The teacher and the learning environment

The teacher's role in establishing a learning environment in a setting which is outside of their control as well as helping the learner deal with the 'four Cs' provides challenges for even the most experienced teacher. However, where there is high synergy between support, direction and structure, 'nurturing environments' provide the settings for changes in values and beliefs as well as the exercise and development of judgement (Atkinson, 2000, p. 55). Because developments in health care are the catalysts for new roles with the consequent movement in role boundaries and the associated 'barricade' response of some professionals, the establishment of nurturing environments is paramount when dealing with work based learning.

Richard Brawn in Atkinson and Claxton (2000, p. 152) suggests that Benner's seven categories of nursing competence are analogous to dimensions of teaching. In each case the professional helps, supports, manages change, monitors quality and implements organisational and work role competencies. This image of the teacher is a million miles away from that of an 'expert' using didactic approaches to 'transmit' knowledge to the less well informed. Teaching in work based learning harnesses the expert knowledge from a variety of sources, directs the learner to those sources and engages with the learner in the learning journey.

It is a given that universally there is a 'knowledge explosion'. In health care the vast array of specialisms generate increasing amounts of research, evidence and information. Keeping up-to-date for teachers of health care professionals either means being a specialist with a narrow but focused area of knowledge or being a generalist with a broader handle on trends, concepts and acknowledgement of change and development. Both kinds of teacher are important and can work in unison for work based learning. However, the generalist is more likely to facilitate learning rather than teach in the traditional sense. Brawn (2000) clearly sees the teaching role emerging as that of facilitator.

The teacher and the learner

It is evident that learners in complex practice situations who are already dealing with service education tensions need carefully planned support to help them cope with their feelings of 'threat' caused by the necessity of reconstruction of personal knowledge and beliefs. The process described by Vygotsky as 'scaffolding' and cited by Bunn (1999, p. 75) in her discussion of different kinds of apprenticeship, involves a great deal of support and encouragement on the part of the teacher at the beginning of the learning journey. The support provided by the teacher is gradually tapered off as the learner becomes more confident. The scaffolding approach can be represented as two wedges, one inverted on the other.

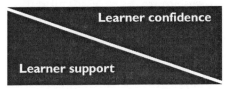

The support will depend upon the point at which the learner starts and the identification by both learner and teacher of the learner's potential, motivation, capacity to learn and learning style. It is important in this kind of learning partnership to clearly define the terms of the partnership to avoid over dependence (of either partner) and/or perceived abandonment. Explaining to learners the feelings they may encounter during learning can never negate those feelings but does to some extent prepare the learner for them and help them to adopt coping mechanisms.

Swallow *et al.* (2000) found that learners felt *'vulnerable and unsure'* and needed *'someone to reassure (them)'*. Scaffolding, for those learners involved shadowing experts, support in dealing with shifting professional boundaries and capitalising on their existing knowledge and professional know-how. Starting from the learners' existing expertise, especially when this is not specific to the teacher, gives the learner a degree of self-belief that grows and gives them intrinsic satisfaction as the learning progresses. The learner is not seen as a blank sheet but as a person with a great deal to offer that acts as a foundation for future learning.

Scaffolding, to be successful, depends on the teacher believing in the potential of learners to develop, the concept of the Zone of Proximal Development (Mahn & Steiner, 2002, p. 46). This concept involves establishing what the learner already knows and can do, then establishing what the learner aspires to learn and assisting the learner to develop confidence and fill the gap. The affective impact on learning takes precedence over knowledge, which, given appropriate resources and direction, the learner can access themselves. The role of the teacher in work based learning is one of partnership, collaborating with the learner and the work place setting plus the professionals who work there, to support the learning experience. Such collaboration needs breadth of vision and the use of the teacher's intuition as well as co-operation and a shared value in the outcomes that work based learning can achieve, plus a belief that the learner can achieve the outcomes negotiated within the partnership.

Theories and a belief that work based learning is the most appropriate approach for the learner and learning involved, are not however, the only consideration. The drivers exerted in HE which include issues of student numbers, widening access and funding impacts on the HE context so that whilst new ways of thinking about learner/teacher partnerships are desirable, there are also targets and resources to consider. There must also be a conviction that collaboration on the part of all the stakeholders, including students, is an imperative without which AWBL would fail to achieve the desired outcome. The HE context for collaboration is discussed in the next chapter.

References

Atkinson, L. (2000) *Trusting your own judgement* in Atkinson, T. and Claxton, G. (eds) *The intuitive practitioner; on the value of not always knowing what one is doing.* (Open University Press, Buckingham, Philadelphia).

Atkinson, T. and Claxton, G. (eds) (2000) *The intuitive practitioner; on the value of not always knowing what one is doing.* (Open University Press, Buckingham, Philadelphia).

Barr, H. (1998) 'Competent to collaborate: towards a competency-based model for interprofessional education.' *Journal of Interprofessional Care* 12 (2) pp. 181–188.

Birchenall, P. (1999) 'Developing a work based philosophy.' *Nurse Education Today* (19) pp. 173–174.

Birchenall, P. (2000) 'Nurse Education in the Year 2000: Reflection, Speculation and Challenge.' *Nurse Education Today* (20) pp. 1–2.

Boud, D. J. and Walker, D. (1991) *Experience and learning: Reflection at work* (Deakin University, Victoria).

Brawn, R. (2000) *The formal and the intuitive in science and medicine* in Atkinson, T. Claxton, G. (eds) *The intuitive practitioner: on the value of not always knowing what one is doing.* (Open University Press Buckingham, Philadelphia).

Chalmers, H. and Bond, S. (1997) *Educational requirements for new nursing roles. Research report.* (Northumbria University and Centre for Health Services Research, University of Newcastle upon Tyne).

Claxton, G. (1984) *Live & learn. An introduction to the psychology of growth and change in everyday life* (Harper & Row, New York).

Coffield, F. (2000) *The necessity of informal learning* (The Policy Press, Bristol).

Cook, S. and Pickard, P. (1997) *Flexible Maths in Flexible Learning in Action* (SEDA Kogan Page, London).

Cope, P., Cuthbertson, P. and Stoddart, B. (2000) 'Situated learning in the practice placement' *Journal of Advanced Nursing* 31 (4) pp. 850–856.

Cowan, J. (1998) *On becoming an innovative university teacher: Reflection in action* (Open University Press, Buckingham, Philadelphia).

Day, K., Grant R. and Hounsell, D. (1998) *Reviewing your teaching.* (Centre for TLA, The University of Edinburgh).

Department of Health (1999) *Continuing Professional Development: Quality in the new NHS* (DoH, London).

Department of Health (2001) '*Working Together – Learning Together*' a *Framework for Lifelong Learning for the NHS* (DoH, London).

Earnshaw, G.J. (1995) 'Mentorship: The student's view.' *Nurse Education Today* (15) pp. 274–279.

Easen, P., Wilcockson, J. (1996) 'Intuition and rational decision-making in professional thinking: a false dichotomy?' *Journal of Advanced Nursing* 24; pp. 667–673.

Eraut, M. (1994) *Developing Professional Knowledge and Competence* (Falmer Press).

Eraut, M. (1998) 'Concepts of competence.' *Journal of Interprofessional Care* 12 (2) 1 pp. 27–139.

Eraut, M. (2000) *Non-formal learning, implicit learning and tacit knowledge in professional work*, in F. Coffield, *The necessity of informal learning* (The Policy Press, Bristol).

Fonteyn, M. and Cahill, M. (1998) 'The use of clinical logs to improve nursing students' metacognition: a pilot study.' *Journal of Advanced Nursing* (28) pp. 149–154.

Harbison, J. (2001) 'Clinical decision-making in nursing: theoretical perspectives and their relevance to practice' *Journal of Advanced Nursing* 35 (1) pp. 126–133.

Knowles, M. (1984) *The Adult Learner: a neglected species* (Gulf Publishing, Texas).

Lave, J. and Wenger, E. (1991) *Situated Learning: Legitimate peripheral participation* (Cambridge University Press, Cambridge).

Liaschenko, J. and Fisher, A. (1999) 'Theorising the knowledge that nurses use in the conduct of their work.' *Scholarly Inquiry for Nursing Practice: an International Journal.* 13(1)

Mahn, H. and John-Steiner, V. (2002) *The gift of confidence: a Vygotskian view of emotions* in Wells, G. and Claxton, G. (eds) *Learning for life in the 21st century.* (Blackwell Publishers, Oxford).

McCutcheon, H. and Pincombe, J. (2001) 'Intuition: an important tool in the practice of nursing' *Journal of Advanced Nursing* 35 (5) pp. 342–348.

McGivney, V. (1999) *Informal learning in the community: a trigger for change and development.* Report of a short DfEE-funded study that focuses on the role of informal learning in starting people on a learning pathway (NIACE, Leicester).

Milburn, A. (2001) '*Working Together – Learning Together*' *A Framework for Lifelong Learning for the NHS* (DoH, London).

O'Reilly, D. (1999) *In conversation with Donald Schon* in O'Reilly, D., Cunningham, L. and Lester, S. (eds). *Developing the capable practitioner. Professional capability through Higher Education.* (Kogan Page, London).

Perry, M. (2000) 'Reflections on intuition and expertise'. *Journal of Clinical Nursing* 9(1), pp. 137–145.

Rogers, C.R. (1983) *Freedom to learn for the 80s* (Charles Merrill, Columbus, Ohio).

Schon, DA. (1987) *Educating the reflective practitioner* (Jossey-Bass, San Francisco).

Spouse, S. (1998) 'Scaffolding student learning in clinical practice.' *Nurse Education Today* (18) pp. 259–266.

Smith, A. (1998) 'Learning about reflection.' *Journal of Advanced Nursing* 28(4) pp. 891–898.

Swallow, V., Chalmers, H., Miller, J. and Gibb, C. (2000) 'Evaluating the development of an Accredited Work Based Learning (AWBL) scheme for A&E nurses.' *Emergency Nurse* 8(7) pp. 33–39.

Swallow, V., Chalmers, H., Miller, J., Piercy, C. and Sen, B. (2001) 'Accredited Work Based Learning (AWBL): Nurses' experiences of two pilot schemes' *Journal of Clinical Nursing – Research in Brief* (10) pp. 820–821.

Swallow, V. and Coates, M. (2004) 'Flexible education for new nursing roles: Reflections on two approaches.' *Nurse Education Today* 4 (1) pp. 53–59.

United Kingdom Central Council for Nursing, Midwifery and Health Working (1999) *Fitness for Practice* (The UKCC Commission for Nursing and Midwifery Education, London).

Winter, R. and Maisch, M. (1996) *Professional Competence and Higher Education: The ASSET Programme* (The Falmer Press, London. Washington DC).

Chapter 2

The Higher Education context: the learners as a stakeholder

Professor Mary Dunning and Hazel Chalmers

Introduction

Drivers for collaboration with employers, potential students, service providers and users in deciding the outcomes of Higher Education (HE) come from a variety of sources. The power base of stakeholders creates challenges for Higher Education Institutions (HEIs). Previously there has been a balancing act between those who provide education – knowing the theory and research and therefore designing a curriculum which is 'fit for the award' – those who commission education who want 'fitness for purpose', and students (perhaps the least powerful but the most important) who want 'fitness for practice'.

Given the change in perspective brought about by the National Committee of Inquiry into HE (Dearing, 1997) and subsequent government policy, HE providers must, in addition, carefully consider their accountability in the use of public funding in line with achieving government targets. The skill for HEIs is to maintain quality of provision whilst at the same time, realising the stakeholder's focus in the most effective, efficient and economically viable way.

Partnership must cease to be a mere buzz word, but become meaningful in the day-to-day negotiation for and provision of education, especially that which is provided for Continuing Professional Development (CPD). Increasingly, and rightly, commissioners want education to meet the needs of developing services in health care. Moreover they want this education to be both practice focused and academically recognised. Some of the drivers including the educational rationale for such recognition are discussed in a conversation with an experienced educationalist and university executive. Educational imperatives are placed in the context of the HE policy environment.

The changing context of Higher Education

A conversation with Professor Mary Dunning, Deputy Dean and Associate Professor for Learning and Teaching in the School of Health, Community and Education Studies. The conversation revolves around the HE perspective of Accredited Work Based Learning (AWBL) in relation to changing contexts and trends.

Q. *What do you think have been the most recent and potent influences on educational policy? What are the drivers?*

A. The first and most influential driver in my view is the number of political imperatives that there are. The present government, since its first term of office has pushed for increasing numbers of 18–30-year-olds to have HE experience. This is the core of widening access and participation. I think that the 18–30-year-old target is narrow because we should be increasing opportunities for those over the age of 30 as well. This imperative is one of four that are influencing priorities for HE funding. Another priority is funding itself, how HE as a whole is to be funded. There is no doubt that the unit of resource within HE has been getting more and more stretched. The notion of publicly funded HE seems to have been reversed over the last few years, by students making a contribution to their HE costs and by reviewing student support monies.

Q. *Do you see a tension there, that on one hand there is a 'push' for widening participation and on the other hand there is the funding issue?*

A. Yes, there is definitely a tension probably illustrated by different universities behaving in different ways. It looks as though the way HE will receive resources in future will be either by students, employers or the public paying. This diversity of funding will challenge the basic tenet of what universities are about. There are to be four major sources of Higher Education Funding Council (HEFCE) funding. One is teaching, the second research, the third widening participation, and the fourth is knowledge transfer, that is selling the assets of university knowledge. There could be extra funding to answer the tension between widening participation and increased costs of HE.

Q. *In relation to these drivers and the philosophy of education – what do you think the impact may be?*

A. I have a personal view that HE in the past was elitist. Twenty years ago only about 10% of the population entered HE. That has changed; I think it is now well over 30%. There was a great difference between what were the old 'red brick' universities with their high research profile and universities that were once polytechnics where the emphasis was largely vocational. It begs the question about the validity of attempting to change all polytechnics into universities, making them the same because in some ways they have been trying to 'catch up'. Perhaps some polytechnics should have stayed with their original missions and what they were formerly intended for. I don't think that they shouldn't have been engaged in research, but they have been pursuing the research assessments when perhaps their strengths lay elsewhere.

Q. *Are you saying that the new universities are 'catching up' that in fact they were aspiring to something that was perceived to be 'better' than what they were doing before and that this increases the divisiveness between vocational education and HE?*

A. I think that the ex-polytechnics wanted the stamp of approval of being able to award their own degrees. They were given their charter and became universities, and partly because of all the pressures in HE including league tables, they have aspired to be the same as the 'red brick' universities. Perhaps along the way they have lost sight of what they were originally intended for. However, in the light of HE funding in future being allocated according to the university's mission, funding will concentrate on a university's strengths. This means that different universities would have different missions and therefore different funding.

One of the most interesting shifts that we have seen within Northumbria University is that links with Further Education (FE) colleges were once 'slightly frowned upon'. Now the University aims to be the key university in the North East of England to have the links with the FE sector.

Statistics have shown that widening participation meant recruiting 'more of the same'. That is an increase in numbers but no change in the student profile. There was little attempt to focus on those who previously would not have aspired to a university education.

The increased emphasis on numbers has encouraged some of the older universities to recruit students from the population that since would have been the market for polytechnics. The drive has been financial, to get the funding. That makes me feel a little uncomfortable because I believe that more individuals should benefit from all forms of education. I believe that this will make our country a wealthier, healthier one and hopefully our population a more satisfied one. So as I see it there is a moral and ethical imperative to widening participation, to involve more people in education and lifelong learning. Lifelong learning is also a relatively new concept emerging within the last ten years.

Q. *What other drivers do you recognise as impacting on HE?*

A. I think the students are different. I think students are now part of a more consumer-orientated society and that they are now dictating and expecting a lot more from HE. I think that this is partly because some of them are paying, and once you pay for something you become a little bit more demanding about it, and of course, for the traditional population, if they themselves are not paying, their parents are. Today's parents and students are much more demanding, much more consumer-orientated, more knowledgeable. They can get more information; they are looking for the quality they expect. The population as a whole is a much more articulate, more demanding population than before.

Also in public sector organisations, their world is changing so rapidly. They can't expect that the knowledge they gained when they got their degree or professional qualification will last them for their entire career. There has to be a way of expanding that knowledge and keeping up-to-date. The populations of lifelong learners – professional people – are going to demand what they want especially because many of them or their organisations are paying for it. They will demand that the learning has relevance to them, this means that there is a tremendous drive for HE to be more accountable. In the past HE was accountable only to itself and I suspect to individual academics – and now of course HE, as Dearing has said, must be accountable to its students and to society. The students who graduate from Higher Education should be fit for the world of work.

Q. *Dearing spoke about employability, flexibility, lifelong learning and portfolios, so what impact do you think that has had on employers?*

A. Are you suggesting that Dearing has actually had an impact on employers or employers are now demanding that the recommendations from the Inquiry into Higher Education Report (1997) should have an impact? I think I would go for the latter rather than the former. I don't think that HE has considered, at this point, the skills including relevant intellectual skills that people need that are essential for their working context. Those skills necessary to be employed and to function in a rapidly changing environment – I am not sure that HE has actually taken that into account yet.

There are still some areas of HE where the updating of employment skills are not taken into consideration as the main priority. There is a need for some 'blue sky' researchers who are going to be at the forefront of knowledge, with the wider thinkers and the 'visionaries'. The people who have well-developed perception, acumen and intuition. For the majority who exit HE, research isn't what they are going to be doing.

I don't think that universities have quite accepted the fact as much as they should, that the majority of graduates need the skills to enable them to 'get on with life'. They (the universities) are going to have to do more. Possible ways to make that happen are the funding and quality assurance bodies making universities more open, more publicly accountable – expecting them to be critically 'looked at' where this has not previously happened. In other words, public information, making the university's information open for public scrutiny, allowing people to ask questions of the university. This is where the work of the Quality Assurance Agency (QAA) has influence... the codes of practice and guidelines, etc. – the new ways of working in HE, implemented by QAA so that the stakeholders of universities can find published information in order to make comparisons between universities.

Q. *You have been talking about universities being more transparent and indicating that the league tables and such things gave people a base-line by which to compare HEIs. I am interested in your views about why employers shouldn't go to colleges of Further Education (FE) for this kind of activity, rather than HE, where FE is much more au fait with NVQs, with BTEC approaches, etc. Why should they come to university, do you think?*

A. I don't see FE and universities as being totally separate, so therefore when you ask me should the employers go to FE or HE I believe that they should go to the place that is able to give them what they require in terms of their expectations. It is a complex world that we live in now. If we look back ten or twenty years there were a lot of basic skills used in industry so workers didn't need the higher competence skills. I think those types of roles are fewer today in society. Many things that people are doing at work today require them to be able to be flexible, to think quickly, to analyse and to look for evidence to inform what they are doing... the intellectual skills, that are usually the outcome of a diploma or degree. I believe that employers and individuals need to begin to give HE some idea of what they require, what they as employers, employees and individuals (because I don't think all the learning should be employment based) need.

Some of the skills and knowledge might be found in FE, some of it might be NVQ level. I am convinced that FE is the right place for provision up to Level 3 and could probably do some Level 4 providing that the people who are supporting the learning, are knowledgeable and are able to teach at the appropriate level.

However, I think that for many of the people in this complex place of work Level 4 isn't going to be enough. They are going to want more advanced skills, and HE is the place where some of those HE skills can be gained. But not in the old traditional way of 'bums on seats' because that just isn't in line with the expectations of the world of work any more, or for individuals with busy lives. So I would see employee development as a progression, a pathway, with some people being in FE and some being in HE.'

Q. *Why do you think we have moved away from 'bums on seats' – why do you think that this School has responded in the way it has to work based learning?*

A. I think this School has probably responded more speedily than other Schools (in this University) because of the stakeholders we deal with. We probably have in this School the largest number of pre-registration/ qualification professional development students in the University. Our student base is not the traditional 18-year-old, coming in for a degree and leaving; perhaps coming back as research assistants or going on to Masters study. The largest proportion of this School's leavers enter the world of work. Many have actually been in that world while they have been taking their undergraduate or their pre-qualification programme. If they are going to come back to the School the majority of them only do so if they see it as a means of improving their working lives and what they do in their employment and/or an opportunity for promotion and salary enhancement.

Self-development is not the only motivation though... most people who work in the public sector or have a vocational role seem to have an intrinsic desire to do their best for the children, clients, patients or whoever they work with. I think that that is a very strong motivation for postgraduate learning. These professionals are part of this School's learning population.

However, that population, is (or will be) working in arenas, where for the last ten years, it was thought that there were too many staff, and therefore student numbers were cut. Then later, there was a sudden realisation that there was a deficit of professionals. In addition to the deficit in the health professions, there is also a deficit in the social care and education professions. Because they have been driven by so many changes people are asking, 'Why on earth be a school teacher?' So there are many professional workers who are working to their utmost in very busy, complex, highly skilled but undermanned organisations.

There has always been Continuing Professional Development (CPD) – much of it because of professional requirements but in the past these people were working in a much less hectic world. It is now so much more difficult for professionals to be released in the old traditional way to attend (the University) for courses one day a week away from their working environment, nor would they consider doing courses that bear no resemblance to their world of work. In addition, many academics are not as in touch with the world of work as the professionals in those arenas.

The other big revolution is that (the University) needs to review traditional modes of delivery. These have changed. There is a dawning realisation that learning doesn't only happen by sitting in the classroom – people are learning at work and in society all the time – probably learning faster than they would in a classroom. Perhaps what they don't have is the opportunity to reflect on that learning, to be able to look for the evidence and use that for reflection. Therefore what is being recognised is this; the world of work has changed, the learners seeking education have changed, and there is much more acceptance of the knowledge and learning that comes from practice. This means a change in the status of practice based learning. Ten years ago if it had been proposed that a student could do a practice project as part of a Master's course, it would have been scoffed at. Certain individuals would have impeded such a development – as an infringement of 'one of the Gods of Higher Education' – the dissertation.

All these "drivers" combine to promote a change of thinking related to the world of work. It is now acknowledged that the body of knowledge emerging from work and the associated learning complements classroom based HE. This knowledge and learning has status, a standard and kudos.

Q. *You have mentioned a number of stakeholders, the institution itself, in this case the School, the employers, the students...*

A. The one not yet mentioned, is associated with a more knowledgeable society. The School provides vocational education therefore the people who are at the 'receiving end' of the service provided by the professionals emerging from the School, that is the service users, patients, children and clients. The public itself is very affected by what happens in the educational process.

Q. *There are very few measures to... show any relationship between education and impact on the public service user. What do you think the gains are for an employer who is commissioning AWBL, or more flexible approaches?*

A. That is absolutely right, but then we haven't tried to get those measures until recently, have we? But if you are an employer, the key thing is that the staff you employ are able to do what you expect them to do... to achieve the end outcome, whatever that might be. For an employer not to have staff who can achieve outcomes in a litigious world is very dangerous. I have always been absolutely amazed how many employers think that education is expensive. It is an old adage, isn't it... about the expense of not having an education, or adult training. I would include training – I am not one of the purists who rejects the concept of training. Any employer who doesn't invest in education and training... in the knowledge and ability of their staff lays them open to potential mishaps and/or losing their employee. Because, at the moment the employee is very marketable... so they will go elsewhere. So what employers can anticipate is having a knowledgeable doer who is also a satisfied member of staff and has loyalty and commitment to what is going on in that sphere of employment.

Q. *Are you suggesting that they also get value for money?*

A. I think they should get value for money but that is such an elusive concept. If value for money means that a project costs less than another but lacks the quality standards then this is where a decision must be made about what it is that is wanted... trying to create a balance between the desired outcome, the cost and the quality. There must be congruence with the skills that are necessary for the output, but the congruence – isn't always possible because money isn't infinite. However, employers don't get value for money from somebody exiting HE with knowledge and skills that bear no resemblance to the world of work. Nor do the employers want education that takes their employees out of the world of work for too long, the kind of learning that is forgotten once the certificate has been awarded.

Q. *What do you think the pluses are for HE in developing flexible learning?*

A. If HEIs do not develop flexible learning, do not take cognisance of these drivers they will cease to exist. They have little choice. A university like Northumbria which is a regional university, albeit with national and international links caters for the greatest part of its population... which comes from the North East of England. If it doesn't take flexibility into account and translate that into change as the world and the geographical area around it changes then in ten years time it could cease to exist. Institutions, perhaps apart from those like Cambridge and Oxford, have little choice. If the HEI is an elitist, high research-orientated university getting plenty of money for research, although there may be some anxieties... finance from teaching and other resources is going to be less of an imperative than perhaps some of the other imperatives that Northumbria University has.

Q. *What about the student... what does flexible learning offer the student? What is in it for the person who comes on to an AWBL programme?*

A. The motivations for the student? They must know it is relevant to them and their work, and beyond. Work based learning, with its specific focus, should include learning that will transfer to other areas in the world of work. In addition for students there is the incredibly strong motivational force to learning... an intrinsic motivation to improve what is perceived as the quality of care.

The other motivation is that HE respects the student's existing knowledge. They value not being seen as empty slates... their experience is not ignored, rather they enter into a partnership... HE using their existing knowledge and experience and working in this partnership to encourage the exploration of the thinking behind ideas and concepts, to enhance that knowledge. But HE teachers cannot be perceived to be the experts in the ideas and concepts about work, rather their role is to encourage students in the educative learning process... using the students' expertise and expanding it. However, HE must optimise the expertise from the student's workplace as well from other relevant professions... so that they are learning with people from their own work environments.

Sometimes the learning is within a team from the same workplace... that is a bonus – as the combined expertise from the team adds value to the learning... so another motivation may be improvement in team working. And for many people as the world of work has changed they realise they have a skills deficit... so work based learning could help in translating new changes and enhance their skill base. It can therefore enhance employees' working roles and skills, their professionalism and their insight into achievements in personal growth within their working environment.

Q. *What might be the negative aspects, or the less attractive aspects – for example, what you have said so far is that it is very work based, it is skill development, personal growth but it is all work focused. Are there any disadvantages to that do you think?*

A. I think there could be a danger that it becomes completely focused in terms of practical skills... to the detriment of the enhancement of those skills at a higher intellectual level. There is a danger of not stopping to think about the evidence behind tasks and not stopping to reflect on the theory that has informed those sorts of actions. The danger of not taking a step back and saying 'we really do need to do some research on this and we could evaluate this – we need to see what is the evidence. There is an awful lot of "gut" knowledge or common sense knowledge, and even intuition... tacit knowledge. Such knowledge has to be critically evaluated in order to learn from it. There is a danger that if all the learning derives from the work environment and is the key driver to the exclusion of reflection and research evidence, rather than being a catalyst, it constrains the learner's potential. There is also a danger of work based learning being seen as an easy option... and it is not an easy option at all.

For both the participants and the facilitators, work based learning is probably more difficult than coming along to university... being given some knowledge, going away, and writing a traditional essay or something similar. Employers may see it as an easy option, because the employee is learning at work. The temptation to think that the employee can continue working at the same pace with no time built in for learning and study. The learners need time to sit back, to reflect within a group; they also need time on their own as an individual learner.'

Q. *What is your vision for the way forward for work based learning?*

A. Recognition... as legitimate learning... legitimately accredited and assessed... its' outcomes viewed with the same level of credence as any traditional provision in the traditional learning and assessment environment. I think Northumbria University is on the way to doing that. There should also be mechanisms to ensure critical scrutiny of work based learning... to allow it to be open for peer scrutiny. To be accepted it is essential it is scrutinised, researched and evaluated... to have standards and external peer review. Another vision is that work based learning must be supported by skilled people. This is a stark development issue if work based learning becomes more mainstream rather than peripheral, which it is at the moment. To become more mainstream means consideration of the academic role and the skills of the people who are involved in delivery. There also has to be access to the evidence required through the appropriate technology. Workplaces and employees within them must not be hampered by limited learning resources. My vision is for technological support, quality standards, critical scrutiny, both in terms of research and in terms of external examining, external QAA processes and, through all, of those universal recognition of work based learning as a legitimate alternative form of university provision.

Reference

National Committee of Inquiry into Higher Education (1997) *National Committee of Inquiry into Higher Education Report* (Chair Sir Ron Dearing) (Newcombe House, London).

Chapter 3

Consultancy and collaboration for 'customised' education

John Miller, Hazel Chalmers and Veronica Swallow

Introduction

The drivers for change in Higher Education (HE) illustrated in Chapter 2 and the following example of collaborative working, compel the 'partners' involved to be explicit and open about their value stance underpinning the partnership. The common ground of values and beliefs must be set out, understood and agreed upon. Each stakeholder, including the Higher Education Institution (HEI), must have clear knowledge of what they can expect, their role and the expectations and roles of their fellow partners.

This University's case for AWBL is predicated upon the following tenets:

- On-the-job learning already happens in many work situations and has little 'external' recognition.
- Lifelong learning, professional development plans and continuous professional development are high on the agenda for most professional regulatory bodies.
- There has been a shift in values associated with competence based learning.
- Reflective practice is an integral part of professional development.
- There is a small but growing body of educational knowledge relevant to learning at work.

- Work based learning is a 'marriage' of organisational learning needs, what the employee needs to enhance their role and what the university can provide in facilitating the match at an appropriate accredited academic level.

These values and beliefs form the bed-rock of flexible education most likely to meet the emerging and changing needs in Continuing Professional Development (CPD) in the National Health Service (NHS). In addition they capture the evolution of the focus on and belief in work based learning as a means of addressing CPD.

In the wake of the National Committee of Inquiry into HE (1997), authors have suggested that a new ethos of working has developed in Higher Education, responding to the need for increased partnerships with stakeholders, especially employers (Chalmers *et al.* 2001). Ayers and Smith (1998) have argued that NHS Trusts need responsive education that meets the diverse requirements brought about by changing health policy and the subsequent development of new nursing roles. The driver to be responsive to stakeholders and to respond to employers with effective solutions has meant that this School has had to reassess the ways in which it relates to employers. The following example illustrates the result of the reassessment.

The School received a request for an educational programme to support skill development for 21 experienced nurses working in Accident and Emergency (A&E) The intention was to prepare the nurses for the role of Emergency Nurse Practitioner (ENP) in order to provide a nurse-led Minor Injuries Unit (MIU). Different from conventional ways of working, this new 'role' initiative would incorporate some tasks, previously the responsibility of medical staff. Traditional university provision in the form of ready-made programmes of study was unlikely to meet these specific needs. The time-scale for the opening of the MIU was approximately a year from the time the request for education was made.

The challenge was to design an academically recognised programme for autonomous practice and associated decision-making to meet the collective and individual requirements of the nurses and address the strategic plans of the Trust. The question that emerged was, would the School need a new model of consultancy or a new way of collaborating to ensure that what we developed was acceptable to all stakeholders? The context in HE was right, the values and beliefs were supportive of innovative developments being mindful of stakeholders' requirements. Was our previous model of consultation appropriate for the changing climate in the NHS?

To integrate collaborative working and consultancy together seemed a most obvious way forward and the work undertaken by Anderson and Burney (1996) in creating a collaborative approach to consultation, which is seen as collegial and egalitarian appeared to reflect our preferred way of working. They describe their framework as a partnership in which consultant and client combine expertise to explore dilemmas and challenges and develop new possibilities for resolving them. The organisational consultation methodology is a way of integrating people and business strategies in building pathways to change and success. The part of Anderson and Burney's framework, which reflects the way we want to work with stakeholders, is described as the post-modern perspective. It challenges the technical and instrumental nature of consultation and the notion of the consultant as the expert. It favours ideas that the construction of knowledge is through social interaction with knowledge being seen as fluid. The knower and the knowledge are seen as being interdependent in establishing a consultancy and collaboration model with stakeholders. It is, therefore, important to emphasise the importance of language. For it is the language which is the medium in which people create understanding and knowledge with each other through communication. (Anderson & Goolishian, 1988; Goolishian & Anderson, 1987).

From a post-modern perspective, organisational consultation can be viewed as a linguistic event that involves and takes place within a conversational process or dialogue. Dialogue is seen as the essence of the process and entails shared enquiry – a mutual search and co-exploration between client and consultant as well as among those working alongside the client (Anderson, 1995). The shared enquiry is fluid and it encourages new ideas and viewpoints to be advanced in the conversation. In this instance the Trust, the nurses and the School were about to work together to meet the educational need, therefore, establishing clarity in communication and action was essential.

As consultants, our aim was to create a dialogue to explore ideas and to facilitate further discussion. Anderson (1995) has suggested that we should assume a philosophical stance in such a relationship, adopting a way of thinking about, acting and responding to people. The stance is characterised by an attitude of openness, respect and curiosity towards the client and their needs. Our consultation began with an interview with the Head of Nursing, which centred on his objectives and the need to establish a nurse-led Minor Injuries Unit. During the consultation it became clear that there were different perceptions of what constituted the new nursing role and therefore what the learning needs might be. Another issue evident in the interview was that there were different perceptions of what AWBL entailed. Although as consultants there may be an initial structure or outline for the consultation, it is wise not to operate from a set agenda or with preconceived ideas concerning the direction that the conversation should take or what the outcome would be. The task is to create and continue the dialogue and discover with the client what is significant.

In this case as consultants we were more interested in the clients' ideas about his or her organisation and the manner in which it operates than in proposing our own ideas. This conversational style and attitude entailed a natural curiosity about the potential dilemmas and a desire to acquire understanding. Consistent with what Anderson and Burney (1996) suggest, we listened actively to the narrative being presented to ensure that there were as few misunderstandings as possible. We continuously checked out what we thought we heard. By operating in this manner during a number of meetings with the Head of Nursing, the nature of the consultation changed from a hierarchical, and interventionist relationship between an expert and non-expert to a collaborative and egalitarian dialogue between people with different types of expertise.

As consultants we assumed the role of facilitators of the dialogue regarding the concerns of the client, in this case the Head of Nursing, instead of experts expected to provide solutions. As we became conversational partners with our client, the dialogue was able to explore new ways of thinking and acting regarding dilemmas, problem-solving and communications. Moreover, the direction being jointly agreed upon was appropriate in relation to the contextual issues in both organisations.

Following the interview with the Head of Nursing it was decided to consult with the nurses who would eventually become Emergency Nurse Practitioners (ENPs). What were their perceptions of their learning needs? Our intention was to use the collaborative inquiry philosophy to create a dialogue and stimulate conversation focused issues generated by our clients (Anderson, 1995). The aim was to attempt to engage them in CPD, optimise on their current clinical expertise and reduce any apprehension they may be experiencing as part of the role change.

Whilst there was mutual agreement that it was possible and desirable to work together to meet the learning needs, a true collaborative partnership had not been established at this point with all interested stakeholders in the organisation. What had not been clear was the explicit nature of the new role. Two days of workshops were held using the collaborative inquiry philosophy. These led to a clear picture of the nurses' existing A&E roles and the skills they aspired to achieve for their new role. Thus the School and the nurses also became conversational partners.

The focus of the learning which emerged was of anticipated interventions associated with the minor injury most frequently encountered in the A&E department, i.e. injuries of the lower limb. The skills needed in this context and in particular to help them judge whether nursing or medical intervention was the best course of action for the patient were; patient examination; history taking;

assessment of health status and decision-making. Following this, a series of related topics emerged which were incorporated into themes. These themes were:

- Clinical issues
- Theoretical issues
- Legal issues
- Communication and documentation
- Professional boundaries
- Evaluation.

Northumbria University staff also introduced the nurses to the fundamental features of negotiated learning; reflection and learning contracts. The consultancy had moved from information gathering and sharing, to University staff generating proposed solutions. The first phase would be to develop the learning environment, design in detail the learning programme and negotiate with the nurses their specific learning outcomes. In the belief that the clinical issues were being resolved in parallel with the creation of the learning programme an AWBL framework was created. The framework was designed to provide a structure to the learning process, to facilitate the incorporation of the same standards as conventional university based programmes, whilst enabling the nurses to articulate and take ownership of their own learning in the workplace. Within the framework four phases were created:

- Profiling and identification of learning themes, which entailed the identification of existing learning and experience, future learning needs and potential for achievement of academic levels.
- Development of learning contracts, which involved group and individual tutorials to facilitate the development of learning outcomes specific to the learner, and the incorporation of learning outcomes into a learning contract.
- Knowledge, understanding and skill development, involving seminars, tutorials to monitor implementation of the learning contract, negotiated practice experience and independent study.
- Assessment and accreditation.

Whilst the learning centred on the development of nurses, it was realised that it would be crucial that the new nursing role of the ENP was clearly defined and accepted by co-workers. In addition, it became apparent that collaboration with other professionals whose roles were typically associated with contributing to care for patients in A&E was an essential element of a successful outcome.

A meeting was arranged by the Head of Nursing to discuss the intentions of the programme with four A&E consultants. Whilst the most senior had previously been discussing the initiative with the Head of Nursing, this was the first meeting with Northumbria University staff. The timescale of eight months appeared to create unwanted pressure for three of the consultants, who expressed grave doubts about the feasibility of being involved as teachers/assessors in the programme. The full impact of the new role on medical staff had not been foreseen. Many of the medical staff had in the past, provided some skill development for nurses in A&E. However when it came to formal commitment to the nurses' learning the time and effort necessary were highlighted. University staff were concerned that if medical staff did not support the programme the relevant skill development could not take place. It was also feared that the concerns of the medical staff could be transmitted to other professionals, for example, the senior pharmacist and radiologist who could potentially contribute to the learning.

A delay in having agreement of the input from professional colleagues, which hinged upon their time and reimbursement, delayed the seminars starting. It became crucial to establish an infrastructure to manage the implementation of the education, to create the necessary learning environment and to support the nurses in their learning and ultimately in their new roles. Although some medical staff had expressed reservations, it was hoped that through further negotiation and the commitment demonstrated by most of the key players their support could be gained ultimately.

A Project Management Group (PMG) was set up with Northumbria University staff, the Head of Nursing and the senior A&E consultant. In time two A&E nurses also joined the PMG. The involvement of the consultant was to help in clarifying the new nursing role in relation to medical roles. The multi-professional participation also improved shared understanding of the project and eventually enhanced collaborative learning and working. Project management did, therefore create closer partnerships and facilitate understanding of a common process. It also helped in clarifying the key personnel in relation to the programme. The further discussion and negotiation led to medical colleagues taking responsibility for:

- Leading the development of clinical protocols
- Providing clinical seminars
- Providing opportunities for clinical shadowing and opportunistic learning
- The design and implementation of clinical skill assessment.

Without this collaboration there would not have been the confidence in skill development. Certainly more issues arose as the project unfolded, but a way of working had long been established that was collaborative and could be seen within a consultancy framework.

Collaboration in developing work based learning, according to Waddington and Marsh (1999) is based on collaborative relationships. They also state that shared responsibility for planning and creating the learning process are key features of experiential learning. Chalmers *et al.* (2001) discuss the development of this project and state that collaboration was eventually crystallised through the formation of the Project Management Group. This is certainly true when considering the working together of all stakeholders, but as this chapter suggests collaborative working and consultancy were a key feature of the initial process when Northumbria University staff met with the Head of Nursing and subsequently the nurses to identify learning needs.

Collaboration continued throughout the design, implementation and evaluation of the AWBL. The next chapter explores this collaboration from the Trusts' perspectives.

References

Anderson, A. (1995) *Effective Marketing Communications; a skills and activity based approach* (Blackwell Business, Oxford)

Anderson, H. and Burney, J.P. (1996) *Collaborative Enquiry: a post-modern approach to organisation consultation in changing organisations* (Karnac Books, London, New York).

Anderson and Goolishian (1987) 'Language Systems and Therapy: an evolving idea.' *Journal of Psychotherapy* 24 (3s) pp. 529–538.

Anderson and Goolishian (1988) 'Human Systems as Linguistic Systems; preliminary and evolving ideas about the implications of clinical therapy.' *Family Process* (27) pp. 371–393.

Ayers, S. and Smith, C. (1998) 'Planning flexible learning to match the needs of consumers, a national survey.' *Journal of Advanced Nursing* (27) pp. 1,034–1,047.

Chalmers, H., Swallow, V. and Miller, J. (2001) 'Accredited Work Based Learning: an approach for collaboration between Higher Education and practice.' *Nurse Education Today* Nov 21(8) pp. 597–606.

National Committee of Inquiry into Higher Education (1997) *National Committee of Inquiry into Higher Education Report* (Chair Sir Ron Dearing) (Newcombe House, London).

Waddington and Marsh (1999) 'Work Based Learning: Implications for team and practice development.' *Advancing Clinical Nursing* Mar 3 (1) pp. 33–36.

Chapter 4

Collaborative working: the service perspective

Chris Piercy and Bas Sen

Background

The National Health Service (NHS) in the UK was established just over 50 years ago and was in 1995, according to Levitt, Wall and Appleby, the largest organisation in Europe. It is recognised as one of the best health services in the world by the World Health Organisation but there is a continuing need for improvements to cope with the demands of the twenty-first century. In recent years the most radical proposed changes were outlined in *The NHS Plan* (DoH, 2001). The biggest concern people have about the NHS is the wait for treatment, be it for emergency or elective work. It has long been recognised that the rate limiting factor regarding Accident & Emergency (A&E) departments' (formerly known as casualty departments) attendees is the volume of patients versus the availability of medical staff. However, according to Calman (1997), Tye (1997), Tye *et al.* (1998), Sakr *et al.* (1999) the majority of patients do not require the attention of doctors but need access to professional advice.

These facts, combined with strategies to address the Patients Charter (1991), measures to reduce junior doctors hours and recommendations of an Audit Commission report, have been responsible for the emergence of Emergency Nurse Practitioner (ENP) roles in the UK. Together with the creation of NHS Direct; both nurse-led services have given certain patients the opportunity to access the health care system rapidly but without overloading the emergency care system. Balancing demand by streaming patients to appropriate practitioners is not a new concept and has been done with success as far back as the 1950s in China (Barefoot Doctors) but introducing the concept in Britain has been a fundamental NHS change.

In the 1990s it was recognised by senior staff working in the A&E departments in Newcastle upon Tyne that the number of complaints relating to patient waiting times were growing. This along with the constant drive to reduce waiting times, by the Health Authority and Department of Health (Patients Charter 1991) was a persistent thorn in the side of the A&E nurses. There was a genuine belief that some changes to the way clinical practice was organised and care delivered would significantly improve the situation and there was a strong commitment to this amongst the staff. Nursing staff from the A&E departments in Newcastle upon Tyne had heard about the emerging role of the ENP and believed the development of such a role would help to significantly improve waiting times locally, whilst also increasing job satisfaction. This view was later supported by the Audit Commission (1996), who suggested that it may be necessary to change the current pattern of A&E services in order to maintain the present quality of care. The report endorsed the development of ENP roles and highlighted the need to move from a purely 'medical model' of care to an integrated service, which could be partially nurse-led.

During 1997, discussion papers were developed for the Trust Board to outline suggestions for changing the service. The Board was sympathetic to the suggestions but felt the time was not right for such a change. The city was facing a huge change to the provision of Acute Services as a result of the Acute Services Review (ASR, 1994) and this would ultimately result in the closure of one of the main hospitals by 2005. This was proposed as a way of ensuring the efficient and rationalised provision of general, specialist and tertiary services across the city. The ASR also supported the notion of one A&E department for the city that would be supported by a satellite nurse-led Minor Injury Unit (MIU). The other concerns voiced by the Trust Board related to the time that it would take to educate the required number of ENPs. The only educational programmes available at that time were at degree or Masters level and would take two years for each practitioner to complete. There was a belief that if this type of educational preparation was introduced the existing service would suffer as a result of time spent away from clinical practice by the senior nursing staff.

The drive by the Department of Health (1991) to implement measures to support the reduction of junior doctors' hours also added pressure to an already stretched A&E department. The department had more than 100,000 attendances per year (and rising by a rate of 1–2% per year). Of these attendances more than 80% could be categorised, using the Manchester Triage System, as 3, 4, and 5 (patients with minor injuries/illness). Senior nursing and medical staff from A&E believed this was the right time to plan and implement a change. Because of the urgent and varied nature of their working environment, A&E nurses have been described as being multi-skilled. For many years they have dealt with all types of clinical emergencies. It is frequently the nurse who determines the triage category of each patient on arrival in the department. What was now needed was to take this service one step further; to formally enable the nurse to assess patients by taking full histories, taking into account any signs and symptoms noted, request and interpret investigations, make an initial clinical diagnosis, commence treatment and discharge the patient if relevant or alternatively refer to the appropriate medical practitioner.

The lack of flexible learning to support the development of ENPs was a catalyst in the development of a collaborative approach by Northumbria University and the Newcastle upon Tyne Hospitals NHS Trust. A joint bid was submitted to the Northern and Yorkshire Regional Health Authority for non-medical education and training funding to support the development of 21 experienced and senior A&E nurses to ENP roles using a process of AWBL. The bid coincided with a merger of the two acute Trusts in the city. One Trust was located in the city centre – the other in the west of the city.

The newly merged Trust Board revisited the Acute Services Review and considered the best way to ensure the 21 nurses could achieve ENP training with as little disruption to service provision as possible. It was soon recognised that the best way forward was to reconfigure A&E services across the city and provide a service from one site only, the preferred site being in the city centre. To achieve this goal would require a radical review of service provision and a short-term location to a site in the west of the city. A strategy was drawn up as shown in Table 1.

Table 1.

Service	Medical/nursing input	Location	Rationale
A&E – for the most medically urgent cases	Doctor-led input	City Centre	Access to core medical and surgical services
Minor injuries unit. For GP emergency referrals	Nurse-led	City Centre	Direct access, referral to A&E if required
Walk-in centre	Nurse-led	West of the City	Direct self-referral

Short- and medium-term measures were necessary to counter threats to the strategy such as:

- Potential removal of accreditation for the education of junior doctors. This would reduce the service input of junior doctors. Measures to improve the education prevented loss of accreditation.

- Demolition of large parts of the city centre site to enable a Private Finance Initiative (PFI) to progress. A&E was temporarily moved to the west city site.

- Time to release nurses for education and training as ENPs and set up nurse-led services.

The proposed change of location of the A&E department from the city centre to the west presented a new opportunity to introduce the role of ENPs who could respond to the challenge. The plan was to admit GP emergency referrals directly to the appropriate speciality in the Trust rather than to filter them through A&E. This would enable A&E to provide a more focused service to those accessing the department. The development of a MIU on the city centre site was crucial to the success of this plan. At the same time the Department of Health announced its intention to pilot the development of nurse-led 'Walk-in Centres' (WIC). A bid to develop such a service was prepared and accepted for a WIC in the west of the city, the longer term strategy being to relocate A&E in the city centre. This together with the WIC in the west could together provide a comprehensive service.

The pressure was then on to employ two ENPs within one year. It soon became apparent that nurses with appropriate training where not available locally, so we were unlikely to recruit fully educated and competent nurse practitioners. A small number of Primary Care Practitioners were recruited to work in the WIC, however, there remained a short fall in the number of nurses able to independently manage the care of patients with minor injuries.

The joint bid to the Northern and Yorkshire Regional Health Authority for Non-medical Education and Training funding was approved. This enabled the collaborative partnership with Northumbria University, outlined and discussed in Chapter 3. An interesting journey was to begin.

This was the first time such a project had been undertaken by Northumbria University and the Trust. It was to require complete collaboration and commitment from medical, nursing and academic staff to ensure its success. Whilst the vision was clear the method was not. The role and motivation of each discipline was to present some challenges in the coming months. These challenges enabled significant personal development and professional growth of the participants. The importance of clear and concise communication became apparent.

The journey begins/developing the project

Approval of the bid was in fact to be the easy part of the process.

According to Brennan and Little (1996), any work based learning which is going to be explicitly recognised through the award of academic credit needs to be set within some kind of framework which will assist the process of making explicit and articulating the knowledge and skills being consolidated and developed by the learner in the workplace. With this uppermost in our minds we embarked on what was to become an exciting journey.

The shared vision by all those involved was the development of two ENPs from the existing workforce of senior and experienced A&E nurses. In practical service terms it was not possible to achieve this for all two in a single cohort. The selection of participants was undertaken by the Head of Nursing, Senior Sister and the Senior Consultant in A&E. It was decided to offer the opportunity to all A&E nursing staff who at that time were employed at grade F or G. The first 12 nurses were identified without formal interview. Each of the nurses had different academic achievements ranging from little previous formal involvement with academic development to a Masters degree.

The first step was to agree the competencies required by nurses once they became ENPs and map these against their current competencies. This was achieved through profiling and the creation of individual learning contracts and later on the development of portfolios of evidence of achievement.

A Project Management Group (PMG) was established with representatives from the University and Trust (medical and nursing). The purpose of this group was to oversee the development of the programme and to ensure adequate facilities and support were available for the participants. Chalmers *et al.* (2001) highlighted the importance of clarifying responsibilities of the PMG to ensure effective achievement of the goals.

The new skills required by the nurses related to history taking, the examination of injuries covering upper and lower limbs in the first instance, to be followed eventually by skin conditions, ear, nose throat and eye conditions for adults and children over the age of 12 years. Box 1 illustrates the learning outcomes developed for the nurses and reflects the fact that the nurses were working at academic level[1] 2 or 3.

Box 1.

Level 2   Learning outcomes

At the end of the scheme the participant will be able to:

- Demonstrate that existing skills have been developed and augmented by new skills which will contribute to the ENP role.
- Demonstrate, using evidence, competence in role development which indicates problem-solving abilities.
- Discuss the themes identified in the Learning Contract, giving examples which demonstrate understanding.
- Apply a model of reflection in the analysis of learning experience.
- Identify relevant theories, research and sources of evidence which have supported role development.
- Discuss the potential for further role development specific to the ENP role.

Level 3   Learning outcomes

At the end of the scheme the participant will be able to:

- Demonstrate that existing skills have been developed and augmented by new skills which will contribute to the ENP role.
- Demonstrate, using evidence, competence in role development which indicates problem-solving abilities, critical thinking and decision-making.
- Critically discuss the themes identified in the Learning Contract, giving examples which demonstrate appropriate synthesis.
- Apply a model of reflection in the critical analysis of learning experience which indicates potential for reflecting in and on practice.
- Discuss relevant theories, research and sources of evidence which have supported role development.
- Identify examples of theories, research and sources of evidence which have potential to support further role development.
- Discuss the potential for further role development specific to the ENP role.

Communication between the management group members was haphazard in the first instance with assumptions being made about the role of Northumbria University staff and the Trust staff. This resulted in some tensions in the early days as the Trust staff had been under the impression Northumbria University staff would be developing the curriculum and organising both the delivery of the theoretical input and assessment.

Progress was slow until realisation of the situation was apparent. The PMG became more focused and agreed to meet fortnightly to plan the curriculum together also to agree the assessment process together. This was particularly crucial, as it had been agreed the standard of competence achieved by the nurses had to be the same as medical staff undertaking the same duties. Clearly the reliance on senior medical practitioners at this point was crucial to support the participants in the workplace by providing supervised practical experiences along with the theoretical input in relation to clinical examination of the patients.

Having agreed our expectations of each other the management group was now set to deliver the project with extremely tight deadlines. A project plan was developed with clear milestones and time-scales, which enabled more focused debate to take place. A starting point was to ensure the participants understood the legal and ethical implications of their new roles and compliance with the UKCC – Code of Professional Practice (1992) in relation to role expansion.

The enormity of the task was underestimated by all concerned; practitioners, managers and educators alike. After the initial enthusiasm settled the fact that this project was pushing the frontiers of nursing practice in Britain to new heights was realised.

During an early management team meeting it became apparent that the need for evidence based protocols had been overlooked. This presented significant problems, as these protocols would be required to inform the learning process. A mammoth task lay ahead to develop protocols which were not only evidence based but were also agreed by the various medical staff from across the specialities to whom the ENPs would be referring. A draft set of protocols was piloted for the first cohort. These were amended in light of the findings both during the delivery of the theoretical sessions and following comments from the medical staff. It was important the protocols reflected current up-to-date practice to minimise any possible clinical catastrophe.

Having agreed the draft protocols and the content of the programme, the AWBL process commenced. Each nurse was supported by a clinical mentor and academic supervisor to develop personal learning outcomes relating to the generic outcomes outlined in Box 1. These learning outcomes became the basis for individual learning contracts. At the onset the participants were enthusiastic and keen to learn, each recognising their existing level of skill and knowledge and articulating the learning that they needed to undertake in order to achieve their learning outcomes. The nurses soon identified concerns about their ability to work as ENPs. As their knowledge increased they became more concerned.

Benner (1984) has described this as novice to expert; it was remarkable how the work of Benner could be witnessed in reality so clearly.

There was a period when the participants resented the protocols because they tended to interpret them in 'black and white'. If the protocol indicated an action or intervention then this had to be undertaken. For example, there was a genuine concern on the part of the medical staff that antibiotics may be given unnecessarily as there was no degree of deviation from the protocol allowed. This adherence to 'rules' is a recognised stage in the learning and development process according to Benner (*op. cit.*).

The need for medical mentors presented another challenge. Despite their having agreed to the principle it was difficult to engage senior medical staff in sufficient numbers to support the learning in clinical practice of the participants. The responsibility fell to a few truly committed individuals. It was recognised this issue would be resolved with subsequent cohorts because as the first cohort became expert ENPs they would, in time, be able to support the learning of subsequent cohorts in the clinical environment. The pace of learning and the need to treat each participant as an individual also had its impact. The support issues were facilitated by learning from the Leading an Empowered Organisation (LEO) programme, undertaken by Chris Piercy while this AWBL development was in progress. Recognition of treating each participant as an individual, taking account of their previous experience resulted in each participant requiring different levels of support and direction.

It was decided to structure the learning into modules focused around the needs of particular client groups. The first module dealt with minor injuries to the upper and lower limbs. Subsequent modules would include eye; ear, nose and throat followed by skin complaints and women's health issues. Each module would last for approximately six months. The plan was that the ENPs would be able to practice without direct supervision as soon as successful assessment had been achieved; this was to ensure learning was not lost by lack of practice to maintain competence. To be successful the ENPs needed to be able to request radiological examinations and to administer various medications such as analgesia and antibiotics via Patient Group Directives rather than having to refer back to a doctor. However, initially this was not well received by some of the radiologists and radiographers. Clinical assessment of the ENPs was similar to that of junior doctors and included Objective Structured Clinical Examination (OSCE) along with the completion of academic assignments.

In the early days of the AWBL, medical staff who had received referrals from ENPs expressed concerns. This was based on the impression that an increased number of inappropriate patient referrals had been made to other specialities such as fracture clinic. An audit of this was undertaken and found to be the same as the practice of new junior doctors. Subsequent audit revealed a greater degree of appropriate referral by the ENPs. This continued to improve as their level of competence and confidence grew. Audit also highlighted a reduced incidence of missed fractures by the ENPs when compared to junior doctors. This finding reflects the work of Barr *et al.* (2000) who concluded nurse practitioners are as competent as casualty officers in reading radiological films.

It was decided that the ENPs would have dual roles to maintain their competence across all areas of practice within the A&E, MIU and WIC. However, it soon became evident that the needs of the patients attending the WIC were not being met. The decision to allocate specific ENPs to the WIC was agreed. This gave rise to the opportunity to further develop their primary care skills enabling them to see patients with minor ailments as well as minor injuries. At the same time the Primary Care Nurse Practitioners (PCNPs) were able to access education to support their learning and practice with patients presenting with minor injuries. This has enabled a fully integrated team to be developed which can undertake a wider range of duties than had previously been considered. The rotation of nurses between A&E and the MIU has been maintained. The CPD of this group of nurses can now be effectively addressed.

The process undertaken proved to be rigorous and gave each practitioner academic accreditation for their learning. The credits awarded allowed advanced standing for relevant university awards such as diplomas or degrees with some of the ENPs gaining direct access to Masters' degree programmes.

The outcome from the perspective of the service delivery has been a significant reduction of waiting times for those patients classified as having minor injuries or ailments. Previously these patients were put to the back of the queue when a patient with a more serious injury arrived in A&E requiring medical intervention. A consequential reduction in complaints has also been noted.

The new nursing role is now firmly established. However it must be remembered that this was introduced as a measure to ease pressures on an overburdened system. The full potential of this highly skilled group has yet to be recognised and further developments are underway. Pitfalls are numerous as in the development of any new group of professionals. The need to recognise that their roles need clarity, ongoing professional development and a progressive career structure is an imperative or there is a danger of these hard-working people being forgotten once the government's immediate purpose has been achieved.

Lessons learned during the journey

Many lessons have been learned along the journey:

- Have a clearly articulated plan at the onset, which outlines the expectations of all involved.

- Prepare in advance of embarking on the project to ensure smooth implementation of the plan. The biggest hurdle to overcome was the lack of evidence based protocols to use during the theoretical sessions and to support the changes in role.

- Use national guidance to support the change of practice, if this does not exist then network and learn from others who have experienced the changes. You can save time by learning from others to prevent making unnecessary mistakes, which can prove to be time consuming.

- Involve all professionals in the planning of the project. To agree plans and discover other professionals do not support the changes is time consuming and unnecessary.

- Select participants on their desire to change roles. The result of limiting this project in the first instance to F/G grades put additional pressure on a number of staff in these grades who felt an obligation to undertake this education programme. Others in this grade felt disadvantaged with promotion prospects, as they preferred the traditional role of F/G in A&E. There is a place for both.

- Don't underestimate the amount of time required to support the participants during a period of significant change. Remember not everyone agrees with the proposed changes.

- Give praise and celebrate success at each stage of the process.

- Plan for the future and consider the full impact of the role change across the service.

- Ensure you consider the impact of the change on future recruitment and retention. Experience has shown us that fully competent Nurse Practitioners are a rare commodity, we have lost some along the way to other health care organisations.

- How will you ensure succession planning? No point in developing a service and raising an expectation if this cannot be sustained long-term.

- Review the service dimensions and capacity on an annual basis, assessing the outcomes against the intention.

- Never assume anything – always find out the facts!

Journey ends

We were successful in developing an ENP service, which was supported by the University and the Trust Board. The flexible approach enabled the original service to be sustained whilst skills and knowledge were being acquired to support the changes to the delivery of emergency services across the city.

The fact that this programme led to academic accreditation made the changes more acceptable to all. We were able to demonstrate the robust nature of the new service, which was evidence based and reduced clinical risk to patients. Whilst enabling the delivery of a more responsive service to seriously injured or ill people in A&E we were able to reduce the waiting times for those with minor injuries from more than 4 hours to under 30 minutes.

This method of preparing staff and influencing clinical practice has now been embedded in developments of many types across the organisation. The benefits have included the building of relationships across service providers and Higher Education Institutions resulting in a reduction in the education and practice gap. An understanding of the needs of both institutions has emerged. Since this project commenced opportunities to work collaboratively on research and practice development projects have arisen. Joint presentations at National Conferences have been undertaken again truly demonstrating the benefits of such collaboration.

It is felt this journey will not end, the road ahead is more likely to offer further opportunity for collaborative working in response to the needs of patients, also demonstrating a commitment to the principles behind the NHS plan.

Note

[1] Since the publication of the framework for HE qualifications in England, Wales and Northern Ireland (Quality Assurance Agency, 2001), these levels have been changed to Level 5 and 6, the second and final year of an undergraduate programme respectively.

References

Audit Commission (1996) *By Accident or Design: improving A&E services in England and Wales.* (Audit Commission, London).

Barr, M., Johnstone, D. and McConnell, D. (2000) 'Patient Satisfaction with a Nurse Practitioner Service'. *Accident and Emergency Nursing* (8) pp. 144–147.

Benner, P. (1984) *From Novice to Expert.* (Addison-Wesley, Menlo Park,).

Brennan, J. and Little, B. (1996) *A review of Work Based Learning in Higher Education.* (DfEE, The Open University).

Calman, K. (1997) *Developing Emergency Services in the Community: the final report.* (DoH, London).

Chalmers, H., Swallow, V. and Miller, J. (2001) 'Accredited workbased learning: an approach for collaboration between Higher Education and practice.' *Nurse Education Today* (21) pp. 597–606.

Department of Health (1991) *The Patients Charter* (HMSO, London).

Department of Health (2001) *The NHS Plan* (DoH, London).

Levitt, R., Wall, A. and Appleby, J. (1995) *The Reorganised National Health Service* (5th edn) (Chapman and Hall).

Manthey, M. and Miller, D. (1994) *Leading an Empowered Organisation* (Creative Health Care Management, Minneapolis).

Newcastle and Northumberland HA (1994) *Acute Services Review* (NNHA, Newcastle upon Tyne).

NHS Management Executive (1991) *Junior Doctors: the new deal* (HMSO, London).

Sakr, M., Angus, J., Perrin, J., Nixon, C., Nicholl, J. and Wardrope, J. (1999) 'Care of minor injuries by emergency nurse practitioners or junior doctors: a randomised controlled trial.' *The Lancet* 354 (9187): pp. 1321–6.

Swallow, V., Chalmers, H., Miller, J. (2000a) 'Learning on the job: Accredited Work Based Learning for nurses.' *Emergency Nurse* (8,6) pp. 35–39.

Swallow, V., Chalmers, H., Miller, J. and Gibb, C.E. (2000b) 'Evaluating the development of an Accredited work based learning (AWBL) scheme for A&E nurses.' *Emergency Nurse* (8,7) pp. 33–39.

Tye, C. (1997) 'The emergency nurse practitioner role in major accident and emergency departments. Professional issues and the research agenda.' *Journal of Advanced Nursing* 26(2) pp. 364–370.

Tye, C., Ross, F. and Kerry, SM. (1998) 'Emergency Nurse Practitioner services in major Accident and Emergency departments: a United Kingdom postal survey.' *Journal of Accident and Emergency Medicine* 15(1) pp. 31–4.

United Kingdom Central Council for Nursing, Midwifery and Health Visiting (1992) *The scope of professional practice* (UKCC, London).

Chapter 5

Developing primary health care: a role of Accredited Work Based Learning?

John Unsworth

Introduction

Since its election in 1997 the Labour administration has put in place the most ambitious service development and modernisation agenda seen since the inception of the National Health Service (NHS). This broad ranging programme touches every aspect of health and social care through the development of integrated services and specific programmes designed to improve care for individual groups of service users such as the National Service Frameworks. The NHS Plan (Department of Health, 2000a) and its subsequent planning guidance (Department of Health, 2000b) set out how the modernisation of health care requires not only increased staffing levels but also requires a modern well prepared workforce which is capable of handling change and developing the care they provide. While Higher Education Institutions (HEIs) have responded to some of the needs of the NHS and Social Care organisations for example, by adapting pre-registration preparation for nursing they have struggled to keep pace with such an immense change agenda. This chapter describes how work based learning can be used to meet both the requirements of service development and the need for an adequately prepared workforce. Using case studies related to work based learning programmes within primary and community care the chapter will explore issues around the use of work based learning to meet the needs and demands of health care organisations while at the same time providing a framework for Continued Professional Development (CPD) for the professional engaged in the learning.

Particular issues for primary and community care

The service development and modernisation agenda presents many challenges for primary and community care. Work to meet these challenges is at the forefront of the agenda for the new Primary Care Trusts in England. In some cases the challenges are in part being addressed by collaborative working between the Primary Care Organisations and educational institutions. All Primary Care Organisations are faced with making changes to their services and increasing staff numbers (Department of Health, 2000a), particularly General Practitioners, when the pool of potential recruits is reducing. This combined with an ageing workforce, where 30% of community nurses (Buchan, 1999) and 34% of GPs are over 50 years old (Royal College of General Practitioners, 2001) makes the problems associated with increasing demands, new service provision and meeting government targets appear even more difficult to achieve.

In common with health care providers from the secondary care sector primary care is increasingly looking for creative solutions to allow them to improve access and provide an increasing range of services with the available workforce. This has lead to the development of new roles for nursing staff including the development of nurse practitioners. Pearson *et al.* (1995, p. 157) describes how,

> '... *doctors and managers here, like their colleagues in America before them, have begun to wonder if some more flexible community nurses might be able to cost effectively take on some of the roles they are unable to fulfil adequately because of recruitment problems.*'

Although work to establish a work based learning curriculum for nurse practitioner preparation remains to be done the current nurse practitioner courses already contain an element of work based learning related to clinical assessment. In addition, there is no minimum qualification for individuals who wish to practice as a nurse practitioner and as a result many individuals undertake non-accredited work based education to prepare them for this role. Some work using AWBL has been done in this area already and this is discussed in detail in Chapter 3. Clearly, the preparation of nurse practitioners lends itself to the development of a work based learning qualification which would go some way towards identifying the important part played by health care organisations in developing such individuals.

Another problem related to the ageing community nursing workforce is the availability of suitably qualified individuals to replace them. While some groups of staff for example, district nurses, have low grade staff nurse posts, other groups do not and are therefore recruiting individuals from the secondary care sector who are also experiencing problems recruiting and retaining staff. Following the United Kingdom Central Council for Nursing, Midwifery and Health Visiting work (UKCC, 1994) which established specialist practitioner qualifications at degree level for community practitioners, many Primary Care Organisations were left with a problem in that although they had a pool of new recruits for specialist training many of them did not have prior academic standing to allow them to study at undergraduate level. Again work based learning can be used to develop the current workforce to allow them to progress their careers.

Another issue related to the development of degree level preparation for community practitioner relates to the need to develop the skills and knowledge of the existing workforce so they can cope with the challenges presented by the service improvement agenda. The evolving nature of many community practitioner courses since the 1980s means that the existing workforce are all prepared to different levels with some staff having certificate level qualifications, some diplomas and some ordinary degrees. Work based learning has been used to develop the skills and knowledge of some of these existing staff to allow them to achieve a degree level qualification but more importantly to enable them to develop the skills required to deliver the service improvements desired by the public and the government. The use of work based learning in this context is discussed later in this chapter.

The nature of work based learning

Work based learning owes its origins to the 1980s drive to widen entry and participation into HE and is seen by Evans (2001), as a natural progression from systems such as Accreditation of Prior Experiential Learning (APEL) which focused upon what an individual had learnt through work and life experience. While APEL systems focus on retrospective learning, AWBL concentrates on 'learning while doing' and therefore involves current learning from contemporary practice. It is this feature which makes work based current learning more valuable to employers in that it focuses on contemporary learning and can support both individual and service improvement. Boud, Solomon and Symes (2001, p. 4) describe how,

> '... work based learning is the term used to describe a class of university programmes that bring together universities and work organisations to create new learning opportunities within the workplace.'

There are several reasons why HEIs embrace the philosophy of work based learning. Firstly, it fosters links with employers which has the potential of increasing collaboration between the universities and potential research partners and/or student employers. Such collaboration is particularly important to newer universities who pride themselves on their graduate employment record and their strong links with industry and service employers. Secondly, the universities were required to become more responsive to the needs of employers in preparing the future workforce with the skills and knowledge needed to ensure continued economic growth and development (National Committee of Inquiry into HE, 1997). Thirdly, for some employers, in particular the health service, there is a need to develop more flexible methods of delivery in terms of education which allow individuals to study and learn without the need for lengthy periods away from their workplace. Fourthly, many employers, even those within similar work sectors, have diverse approaches to service delivery and as a result the standard 'off the peg' traditional approach to education can be inappropriate for both the employer and the student. Finally, universities needed to find an approach to education that could cope with the requirement for expedient course development and delivery often required by employers at the cutting edge of service development.

Boud, Solomon and Symes (2001) describe how work based learning programmes typically have six characteristics. The first of these is that work based learning involves a partnership between an external organisation and the educational institution. This partnership arrangement is an important feature as the organisation is required to be more than simply the purchaser of the education for their employees. The organisation needs to put in place systems to support learning within the workplace. Such support may include access to learning resources through information technology and the provision of mentor support for students. In many cases the organisation may be required to provide lecturers to provide specialist teaching input into the taught component.

The second characteristic of work based learning is that the learners within the programme are employees of the purchasing organisation. This can have important connotations for the educational institution because each work based learning programme becomes a bespoke provision, which will invariably drive up the costs and thus can make work based learning more expensive than more generic educational provision. Another element related to drawing learners from one particular organisation means that the work based learning programme needs to be very flexible both in terms of academic level and delivery. It is not uncommon for a work based learning programme to be offered at several different academic levels. This can be challenging for the teaching team but can also provide opportunities for the sharing of skills and knowledge amongst learners at different levels. These issues will be discussed in greater depth later in this chapter.

The third characteristic relates to the fact that the work based learning programme is derived from the needs of the workplace and as a result the work of the organisation or at least an element of it becomes the curriculum for the programme. While this may appear relatively straightforward it can, in practice, require considerable skill on the part of both the educationalist and the organisation link to unpick the elements of the work which need to be targeted. In some cases it is necessary to undertake a mapping exercise to identify the training and developmental needs of the employees before the work based learning programme can be developed. This links with characteristic four, which involves the identification of the learning in which the learners wish to engage. Such learning must be congruent with the views of the organisation related to the skills and knowledge that they have identified as deficit within their workforce.

The fifth characteristic relates to the fact that the majority of learning should take place in the workplace. It is this element more than any other which can provide added value for employers as it often leads to developments within the workplace that enhance the delivery of services or add an extra dimension to the work of the organisation. Boud, Solomon and Symes (2001, p. 6) state that,

> *'... learning is designed not just to extend the knowledge and skills of the individual, but to make a difference to the organisation. Projects are undertaken not just to equip students to contribute to the organisation, but to make a tangible step towards doing so.'*

While the approach to developing services through learning is laudable it is not without its critics. Spencer (2001) identifies that the use of students as change agents can create tensions within the workplace. While some students will be well placed to act as change agents others will not and will encounter resistance. As with change in any context the individual's position within the organisation, political astuteness and length of service are important antecedents to successful change (Clarke, Proctor & Watson, 1998; Manion, 1993).

The sixth characteristic of work based learning programmes is that the education institution is involved in assessing learning against the agreed learning outcomes and awarding academic credit as appropriate. This characteristic allows work based learning programmes to either fit into a framework of continued professional development building to an academic qualification or to use work based learning as the mode of delivery for an entire academic award.

Work based learning as a philosophy covers a wide spectrum of activity from a focus on work based assessment activity within a traditional undergraduate programme to a programme which is entirely focused around learning in the workplace. The case studies describe work based learning programmes that are based in the middle of this spectrum as they encompass work based learning supported by taught university based sessions.

Work based learning to provide multi-professional education

This section describes the development of a multi-agency, multi-professional public health course. Although public health activity with individuals and communities is not a new phenomenon, in the late 1990s there was a fundamental shift in the philosophy guiding such work. The new approaches to public health originated from a change of government and the acknowledgment of a clear link between poverty, deprivation and ill health. This new approach highlighted the need for a 'joined up' approach to tackling health inequalities which has at its centre inter-agency working. The work based learning public health leadership programme was developed by Northumbria University in partnership with North Tyneside and Newcastle Primary Care Trusts. The aim of the programme was to assist health, social care and voluntary organisations to meet the challenges presented by the ambitious modernisation agenda. The Department of Health (2001) state that,

> '... *tackling health inequalities is a high priority for the government and it is a key strand of its modernisation programme designed to develop responsive and effective public services.*'

Practitioners across a wide range of disciplines, from community workers to housing officials are now involved in addressing inequalities and public health issues. This meant that any work based learning programme needed to be multidisciplinary and designed to appeal to several key health and social care agencies from the statutory and voluntary sectors. From the outset the potential learners were identified as practitioners who were involved in identifying health needs and establishing programmes or interventions to address the needs identified.

The programme was designed to be multidisciplinary because of the need to develop the public health role of a range of people from a variety of backgrounds. The programme enabled individuals from different professional backgrounds and services to share experience and skills through taught sessions and action learning sets. From the outset it was hoped that the programme would assist students to develop a greater understanding of each other's role within public health and create some joined up thinking on important local public health issues.

Work based learning was selected as the approach in relation to this development for several reasons. These include the need to tailor the programme to a broad spectrum of students recognising that individuals with a background in housing have a very different public health role to an individual who is a school health adviser. Work based learning was developed in such a way as to it allow the students to structure their learning around their individual role and thus made the programme relevant to a wide range of practitioners. In addition, experience of other forms of public health education acknowledges that a gap can exist between theory and practice. For example, many programmes ask students to undertake a health needs assessment, but once completed this is rarely utilised to its full extent. This work based learning programme was designed to provide added value by encouraging students to demonstrate learning through work based activity which moved beyond simply producing written work for a course. As a result students needed to demonstrate how the needs assessment they undertook was subsequently used to inform public health interventions.

The programme was developed around the three core themes of public health:

- The influence of society, policy and the professions
- Working in new ways
- Leadership and public health.

Each theme was matched to the ten draft national standards for specialist practice in public health (Faculty of Public Health Medicine, Multidisciplinary Forum for Public Health and The Royal Institute for Public Health, 2001), although the programme is designed to provide no more than an introduction to the topic. Students were informed that if they wished to develop a career in public health they would need to go on to study the topic in greater depth and that they may be able to use the academic credit gained through this programme to gain prior standing. The programme was supported by six taught days and five action learning sets. The content addressed during the taught days is outlined in Box 1.

Prior to commencing the programme each student was required to complete a combined application form and profile document. This document had a threefold purpose as it was used not only to identify the appropriate level at which the student would study, but also to identify their entry level knowledge and their expectations of the programme and their own desired learning outcomes. The decision related to which academic level the student would study was made on the basis of prior study, qualification and appropriate experience gained through work. This allowed some students without a first degree to study at a postgraduate level because they were able to demonstrate learning by virtue of their prior work experiences.

Assessment for the programme involved the student compiling a portfolio of evidence related to the learning outcomes. While students were supplied with details of the eight core learning outcomes for the programme each of them was assisted to develop individualised learning outcomes, thus tailoring their learning to their own role within public health. This process involved the use of

Box 1: Content of public health leadership work based learning programme.

Theme One: Public Health: the influence of society, policy and the professions	Theme Two: Working in new ways	Theme Three: Leadership and Public Health
• **Public Health in context** Political ideology Deprivation and the widening health divide Social inclusion Ethnic diversity Universal vs. targeted provision. • **The environment of practice** The political environment Partnership and collaboration Professional and legal issues Managing risk.	• **Working with communities** Planning community based interventions Developing sustainable capacity within the community. • **Health needs assessment** Approaches – epidemiological, rapid appraisal, deprivation assessment Data collection – synthesis and evaluation Deciding priorities Action planning – individual and collective health plans Influencing others to achieve wider health gain. • **Working with individuals** Personality types Helping people change. • **Key areas of public health work** Coronary heart disease Cancer Teenage conception Substance misuse Mental health.	• **Managing time and resources** Finance and health commissioning Project management. • **Developing self** Negotiating and influencing Approaches to reflective practice Career planning Continued professional development. • **Developing others** Building capacity for public health work within other professionals and community leaders Community development approaches.

tripartite negotiated learning contracts which were developed during workplace visits where the student, their workplace mentor and their personal tutor met to discuss how the learning could be related to the students practice role.

Another central feature of the programme was the inclusion of structured action learning. Lee (1999) describes how action learning is not concerned with the accumulation of factual knowledge in isolation from everyday experience. Rather action learning is concerned with the application of real, practical issues, and learning by and from experience. Action learning involves the triangulation of learning from several different sources, including work, books and other learning material and through an action learning set. Action learning is a fluid, dynamic and changeable process that is dependent upon the students, the facilitator and the learning environment for its format and structure. Lee (1999) describes the following characteristics of the process of action learning:

- An action learning set consists of members who offer mutual support and critique in a non hierarchical and equitable environment
- The set adviser ensures an equitable environment is maintained
- Set members take responsibility for their own learning and actions
- Action learning involves doing, trying out ideas, problem-solving, exploring practice issues and reflection.

Within this programme small action learning sets were held between each of the taught days. A structured approach was used to provide a clear framework for discussions and a member of the teaching team facilitated each action learning set. Students were asked to select problems or issues for consideration based

Box 2: Format of action learning sets.

Questions	Meeting format
• Describe your problem in *one* sentence	• Each session lasts 45 minutes
• Why is it important?	• Identification of facilitator
To you?	• Identification of time-keeper
To your organisation?	• Identification of scribe
• What would it look like if it was *fixed?*	• Identify ground rules
• *Who* else would like to see progress?	• Agree who will present their problem/ issue – up to 10 minutes of non-interrupted air time
• *What* steps have you taken so far to resolve this problem?	• Diagnostic phase – questions from students – 10 minutes
• What are the *barriers* to success?	• Suggests for action – 15 minutes
	• Summarise – 5 minutes
	• Problem presenter describes action plan – 5 minutes
	• Scribe hands over notes of questions asked, etc.

upon what had been addressed during the previous taught day. The format of the sessions and the questions used to identify issues are shown in Box 2. The action learning sets were particularly useful to the students as they enabled them to examine the organisation and delivery of public health activity within their own workplace. Gregory (1994) articulates how action learning is useful where individuals are looking not only for academic challenge but also for enquiry related to the world of work.

A total of 30 students were recruited to the programme from three local areas. Each course was made up of individuals from a variety of backgrounds including education, nursing, community workers, allied health professionals, health promotion and medicine. This mixture of students facilitated the sharing of skills and experience and made the programme truly multi-professional. Cook and Drusin (1995) describes how joint education of students who will work together professionally after graduation has been espoused for many years as a way to begin to encourage later collaboration. Inter-professional education is also appropriate for courses that transcend the boundaries of professional knowledge (Hammick, 1998). Both of these factors were considerations in developing a multi-professional public health course as public health knowledge concerns practitioners from a wide range of disciplines including health, community work, education and housing. In addition, the long-term aim of the learning was to encourage more collaborative working.

While traditional course delivery can be used to deliver multi-professional education they often do not have sufficient flexibility to cope with students from several different professional backgrounds (Hammick, *ibid.*). As a result multi-professional education between two or three professional groups from the same service is more common than education for a number of different disciplines from different agencies.

In common with most multi-professional education it was difficult to make the content of the taught sessions applicable to everyone. For example, in some sessions certain people were completely new to the concepts being presented while others had covered this in-depth during prior study or as part of their work role. To some degree this issue could be easily overcome by making the taught sessions optional but this would require the provision of more information about the content of each session so that students could make an informed judgement about whether or not they needed to attend. The original intention of one of the partner Trusts was to develop their cohort of the programme around a specific client group (children and young people) and to recruit solely from two localities within the Trust. This approach would have encouraged greater joint working as it would have brought together individuals who should be working together to provide a coherent set of services for children and young people. Despite the Trust's best efforts, recruitment solely from this group was difficult and to some extent this may have been due to trying to recruit a relatively large number of individuals from a small area. Clearly, allowing a large proportion of the youth and young people's workers to attend a study day at the same time would have a major effect of the provision of services.

Another limitation of the programme related to the lack of continued partnership collaboration once the programme had started. This was a significant oversight on the part of the academic institution and resulted in problems as the programme developed. These problems were quickly remedied but could have been prevented by continued dialogue between the two parties. Another issue related to the health care partners placing the onus on the academic institution to link the taught elements of the programme to the local context. This almost assumes that the purchasing organisation has no part to play in delivering the work based learning. As highlighted earlier in this chapter (see also Chapters 3 and 4) the organisation has a vitally important role in developing opportunities for students to engage in learning within the workplace. To some extent this problem is associated with a perception on the part of the purchasing organisation that work based learning is similar to other methods of educational delivery. As a result, it is assumed that the problem will be less of an issue in subsequent deliveries of the same programme within the same organisation.

The final issue relates to the problematic nature of providing bespoke courses or work based learning programmes and the additional resources this requires. While the focusing of courses/programmes around particular service issues is appropriate this means that each delivery must be specifically tailored to each organisation. As a result the process of planning of both the programme and the individual taught sessions is both labour intensive and expensive. This creates a tension for the academic institution, which has to grapple with the need to be responsive to the needs of employers and the need to cover its costs. Put simply, if organisations want the added value which work based learning has the potential to deliver then they have to pay for it and need to accept that, by its very nature, a bespoke work based learning course will be more expensive than a traditionally delivered course.

Work based learning as part of action research

Work based learning can be used to support the process of introducing change using interventionist research strategies. Using work based learning in this way allows individuals participating in a change to gain academic credit while at the same time developing their skills and knowledge so they can deliver the new service or work in different ways. Meyer (1995) describes how action research is part of new paradigm research, which holds a different philosophical perspective from other more traditional research approaches. As an approach action research is concerned with doing research with and for people, rather than on people. Action research involves the collection of data about a social system while at the same time attempting to make changes to that system through collaborative working with the research students (Hart & Bond, 1995). In this case the study of work based learning was used to develop the skills and knowledge of some of the research students to develop an action research based men's health project.

Early in 2002, Northumbria University was commissioned by the Community Foundation and the Tyne and Wear and Northumberland Health Action Zones to design, deliver and evaluate a project designed to promote men's health. Men's health was selected as the focus for this project because men's health had traditionally been a neglected area (Ions, 2000). The programme entitled '40 Not Out' aimed to promote physical activity and lifestyle change in men from areas of deprivation across Tyne and Wear and Northumberland. The programme involved identifying men reaching 40 years of age and sending them a specially designed birthday card inviting them to attend their local leisure centre for a health and lifestyle assessment. Part of the programme involved developing the assessment skills and knowledge of leisure centre staff, particularly around the area of motivational interviewing so that they would be able to undertake the assessments.

The project involved developing a work based learning programme to address the learning needs of leisure centre staff. The programme was designed to provide a series of taught days prior to the launch of the project followed by a period of work based learning to consolidate the taught days and encourage skill development. The programme was delivered over a six-month period with an initial block of four days early in September to allow the project to be operational immediately after launch. Two further study days were planned three months later.

As described earlier, students completed a combined application form and profile document to identify their entry level qualifications and work related experience. Almost all of the students were drawn from leisure services, although one individual worked within a health promotion department. Again, a wide range of prior academic study was identified amongst the cohort with some students having postgraduate qualifications in Sports Sciences while the majority had vocational qualifications in leisure related subjects. The programme was offered at academic levels of 4, 5 and 6. The wide range of prior study presented challenges for the teaching team as the majority of the students were new to study within HE. All of the students were new to the content of the course (Box 3) although they had been working for many years with individuals who wanted to become more active, motivational interviewing was a new concept. The lack

Box 3: Content of the health and lifestyle work based learning programme.

Theme One: Principles of Assessment and Common Health Problems	Theme Two: Models of Health Behaviour/Health Beliefs	Theme Three: Effecting Lifestyle Change
The assessment process	Key theoretical models of health behaviour:	Basic interviewing skills:
Decision-making pathways	• The health belief model	• Creating trust
Record keeping	• The theory of reasoned action	• Empathy
Understanding Coronary Heart Disease – risk factors, prevention, disease processes, signs and symptoms	• The theory of planned behaviour	• Non-verbal communication
Understanding Stroke – risk factors, prevention, disease processes, signs and symptoms	• The stages of change	• Verbal communication.
Understanding Hypertension – risk factors, prevention, disease processes, signs and symptoms	• Relationship of models to practice.	Motivational interviewing techniques:
Understanding Cancer – risk factors, prevention, specific types prostate, breast, lung, etc. signs and symptoms		• Determining attitudes towards exercise
Understanding Men's Health – specific problems, prostatic disease, signs and symptoms		• Perceptions of health risks and perceptions of barriers and benefits
The nature and scope of prevention programmes		• Intentions and norms
The influence of physical activity on other health and lifestyle factors, e.g. depression, mood, substance misuse, etc.		• The influence of the social context in which the client resides
		• The effect of social support from significant others
		• Work demands
		• Profiling and coping with potential sources of stress.

of prior exposure to HE resulted in a relatively high attrition rate: everyone who commenced the programme continued to attend the study days but many decided not to complete the portfolio for assessment.

Another limitation of the programme was that it was so closely linked to the research project and as a result students viewed the two things as the same entity.

For example, they failed to see how the skills and knowledge developed during the programme could be used in different contexts within their everyday work. In addition, some students felt that they could not continue on the programme if they changed their work role and were no longer involved in the research project. This issue is likely to be a problem for any work based learning programme linked to an action research project.

Another major issue was the fact that the taught component of the programme was compressed because of the need to get the project up and running. This was less than satisfactory for both the teaching team and the students and with the benefit of hindsight a longer lead in time for the project would have been preferred. However, this is often outside of the control of the researcher as it is often set by the project funder.

Despite these limitations this work based learning programme was successful in developing the skills and knowledge of leisure centre staff and assisted the researchers to implement the programme in a short time-scale.

Conclusion

The case studies discussed in this chapter illustrate how work based learning can be used to develop the skills and knowledge of practitioners to prepare them for changes in the workplace as well as to promote service development and collaborative working. Work based learning programmes allow HEIs to become increasingly responsive to the needs of health and social care at a time of unprecedented change. While work based learning is useful within this context for some staff groups others would prefer to study for a qualification or award rather than simply to collect credit points. There is a need to develop programmes that allow students to gain an academic award as well as credit thus making the programme more worthwhile for those staff who may not wish to use credit towards a particular programme.

In addition to promoting service development, work based learning programmes can also be useful in developing the existing workforce, thus addressing the need to develop career pathways for practitioners as well as to ensure that experienced staff are retained and allowed to progress onto specialist practitioner programmes.

References

Boud, D., Solomon, N. and Symes, C. (2001) *New Practices for New Times in Work Based Learning – a New Higher Education?* in Boud, D. and Solomon, N. (eds) (Open University Press, Bucks).

Buchan, J. (1999) 'The "greying" of the United Kingdom nursing workforce, implications for employment, policy and practice.' *Journal of Advanced Nursing* 30(4) pp. 818–826.

Clarke, C.L., Proctor, S. and Watson, B. (1998) 'Making changes: a survey to identify mediators in the development of health care practice.' *Journal of Clinical Effectiveness in Nursing* (2) pp. 30–36.

Cook, S.S. and Drusin, R.E. (1995) 'Revisiting interdisciplinary education: one way to build an ark.' *Nursing and Healthcare* 16(5) pp. 260–264.

Department of Health (2000a) *The NHS Plan: a plan for investment, a plan for reform* (The Stationery Office: London).

Department of Health (2000b) *The NHS Plan implementation programme* (DoH, London).

Department of Health (2001) *Health inequalities: consultation on a plan for delivery* (DoH, London).

Evans, N. (2001) *From once upon a time to happily ever after: the story of work based learning in the UK Higher Education sector* in *Work based learning – a new Higher Education?* in Boud, D. and Solomon, N (eds) (Open University Press, Bucks).

Gregory, M. (1994) 'Accrediting Work Based Learning: action learning – a model for empowerment.' *Journal of Management Development* 13(4) pp. 41–52.

Hammick, M. (1998) 'Interprofessional education: concept, theory and application.' *Journal of Interprofessional Care* 12(3) pp. 323–332.

Hart, E. and Bond, M. (1995) *Action Research for Health and Social Care.* (Open University Press, Bucks).

Ions, V. (2000) 'The trouble with men...' *Nursing Standard* 14(34) pp. 61–62.

Lee, N. (1999) 'Thinking reflectively: solutions through action learning.' *Nursing Times* 95 (49) pp. 54–55.

Manion, J. (1993) 'Chaos and transformation.' *Journal of Nursing Administration* 23 (5) pp. 41–48.

Meyer, J. (1995) 'Stages in the process: a personal account.' *Nurse Researcher* 2 (3) pp. 24–37.

National Committee of Inquiry into Higher Education (1997) *National Committee of Inquiry into Higher Education Report* (Chair Sir Ron Dearing) (Newcombe House, London).

Pearson, P., Kelly, A., Connolly, M., Daly, M. and O'Gorman, F. (1995) 'Nurse Practitioners.' *Health Visitor* 68(4) pp. 157–160.

Royal College of General Practitioners (2001) *Information Sheet 1* (RCGP, London).

Royal Institute of Public Health, Faculty of Public Health Medicine and Royal Society of Health (2001) *National standards for specialist practice: public health* (Healthwork UK, London).

Spencer, S. (2001) *Education for change* in *Developing Community Nursing Practice* in Spencer, S., Unsworth, J. and Burke, W. (eds) (Open University Press, Bucks).

UKCC (1994) *The future of professional practice – The Council's Standards for Education and Practice following Registration: programmes of education leading to the qualification of specialist practitioner* (UKCC, London).

Chapter 6

Developing specialist community practice through Accredited Work Based Learning

Joanne Bennett

Introduction

Changes in health and social care policy over the past decade have clearly impacted on the role and responsibilities of the community nurse. The New Labour Government is committed to modernising the NHS; this being enacted through the modernisation agenda. At the heart of this agenda is the development of a quality service that is integrated around service user needs (DoH, 1997; DoH, 2000a). The pace of change is fast with no signs of a slow down, and the ability to create and lead the changes required of this agenda are clearly dependent upon the knowledge and skills of front-line practitioners, in this case community specialist practitioners (Bennett, 2002; Bennett & Robinson, 2002).

This fact has been recognised by the government who identifies how lifelong learning and the development of all staff is crucial to realising their vision (DoH 2002). Their aim is therefore to ensure that staff are equipped with the knowledge and skills to support changes to practice and improvements to care (DoH, 2000a; DoH, 2001). This chapter sets out to describe how a colleague and myself worked in partnership with the primary care manager and clinical leaders from Gateshead Primary Care Trust to develop a programme of work based learning for community nurses. The overall aim of this was to support these front-line practitioners to develop knowledge and competencies commensurate with their changing role. Prior to describing this process I intend to set the scene through locating the development in both a policy and practice context.

The Context

There are numerous policy documents directing and shaping the modernisation agenda and when unraveled, it becomes clear that they have significant implications for community nurses (DoH, 1997; DoH, 1998; DoH, 1999a; DoH, 1999b; DoH, 2000a; DoH, 2000b). Some of these implications include the need for community nurses to work in partnership with others to:

- identify and explore strategies to meet the health needs of the local population
- address the public health agenda
- develop approaches to integrated care, chronic disease management and intermediate care
- develop nurse-led services
- critically review existing service delivery and skill mix and develop integrated approaches to meeting need, e.g. rapid response teams to meet intermediate care needs
- strengthen the contribution of service users so that they play a key role in the shaping and evaluation of services
- operate within a framework of clinical governance, demonstrating evidence based practice which is delivered within national frameworks
- engage in research and/or practice development
- understand the nurse's role/potential role in the commissioning of services
- identify and plan to meet the education and training needs of the nursing team, linked to the needs of the primary health care team and the organisation
- demonstrate the ability to work with others to lead and change practice (Bennett 2002).

For many, this means critically reviewing existing practice, challenging traditional ways of working and developing knowledge and skills in new areas. This may be particularly so for those who qualified prior to 1994. It was at this time that we witnessed major changes to both pre- and post-registration nursing courses, with the level of pre-registration education becoming a minimum of diploma level and post-registration specialist practitioner education a minimum of degree level (UKCC, 1994). Canham (2002) describes how the thinking behind the 1994 change was centred on the health needs of the population and the preparation of practitioners to meet the needs of health services in the twenty-first century.

Programmes leading to specialist practitioner awards (1994 onwards) were therefore designed to focus on four main areas that would enable the student to meet the demands of their role as a community specialist practitioner through identifying strategies to meet the needs of the community, as well as monitor and improve standards of care through supervision, nursing audit, developing and leading practice, contributing to research and supporting and teaching colleagues (UKCC, 1994; UKCC, 1998). The four areas identified are:

- **Clinical nursing practice** which addresses the development of knowledge and the skills required to meet the specialist clinical needs of patients and carers.

- **Care and programme management**, which focuses on the development of knowledge and the skills to enable the practitioner to seek out the health needs of individuals, families and communities as well as deliver and evaluate strategies to meet those needs. There is a particular emphasis on partnership working.

- **Clinical practice development** which emphasises quality assurance issues such as standard setting, practice development, resource management and effective learning experiences for student's and team members.

- **Clinical practice leadership** that encompasses the development of leadership qualities to address issues such as evidence based practice, practice development and research, staff appraisal, and audit.

Within each area the UKCC identified competencies that had to be met in order to register or record as a community specialist practitioner (UKCC, 1994, 1998; ENB, 1995) (Appendix One).

It is reasonable to assume that practitioners qualifying with a community specialist practitioner award have developed *many* of the competencies required of contemporary practice, and are prepared to meet the challenges of the modernisation agenda, because when the two are compared, there are many similarities, e.g. in areas of leadership and practice development. However, for others, who qualified prior to this, the situation is very different. Many of these practitioners hold the title of a community specialist practitioner but not the award. Depending on when they qualified their preparation was at certificate or diploma level, the preparation being very different to that offered today. While some of this group may have engaged with other forms of Continuing Professional Development (CPD) to update and further develop knowledge and skills, others may not have been afforded this opportunity. It is this group of staff who may need further support to realise their potential.

However, investment in the education and development of staff can be costly in terms of the financial cost of courses and the replacement costs of staff alone.

Indeed a recent Audit Commission review of education, training and development for health care staff estimated that £350 million was spent each year across England and Wales on such activities, which translated to £1 million per year for an average trust (Audit Commission, 2001). The haphazard nature of some of this activity was highlighted together with the need for education and development to be located within the context of the organisation's business plan and the strategic direction of services. Furthermore, when such large sums of public money are being spent on education, both educational providers and purchasers must consider the value of provision in the context of the above and ensure that it is relevant, targeted and focused, encompassing concepts such as lifelong learning. One mechanism to address this is through the development of a learning organisation where personal learning and team development contribute to the delivery of high quality services (Ewan & White, 1996; Pritchard & Pritchard, 1994; Thompson, 1997). The Department of Health (2000a) suggest that work based learning is one way to support this.

It is against this background that a collaborative programme emerged between Northumbria University and Gateshead Primary Care Trust (formally Gateshead Health NHS Trust). The philosophy of this Trust was (and still is) to support all community specialist practitioners (holding the title, not the award) in achieving degree status through either credit accumulation or a degree award. However the Trust had, in the past, expressed concerns about some of the courses in existence, which aimed to meet the CPD needs of experienced community nurses. Among these concerns was the inflexibility of provision, lengthy waiting lists for core units, cost in terms of staff time, and perhaps of most importance, the limited evidence about how learning was translated into practice (Bennett & Robinson, 2001). They therefore wanted some form of educational provision that was flexible, delivered in the workplace, prepared health visitors and district nurses for their changing role whilst at the same time enabled them to acquire academic accreditation. The AWBL programme that emerged was designed to meet those needs, building on previous collaborative work between the two organisations (Bennett & Robinson, 2002, 2003).

Accredited Work Based Learning

Initial enquiry into the strategy indicated that there are many advantages to flexible work based learning. As well as allowing learning to take place on the job and hence reduce the amount of time away from the work place, the process can promote theoretical analysis, personal and professional growth, and the development of thought-related action and reflective evaluation (Birchenall, 1999). For this to happen work based learning must be set within a framework which explicitly states the knowledge and skills being developed by the practitioner (Brennan & Little, 1996). The impetus for us using this approach came not only from these reported benefits but perhaps more importantly from colleagues at Northumbria University who had pioneered it in other areas of practice and produced a set of AWBL guidelines for other staff to use (Swallow, Chalmers & Miller, 2000). Furthermore, they were very willing to share their expertise and learning, providing us with the guidance and support needed to embark on this very different journey.

The Project

A Community Nursing Senior Lecturer and myself initially met with the Primary Care Manager and Clinical Leaders from the Primary Care Trust to explore options to support a cohort of seven practitioners (three District Nurses and four Health Visitors) to achieve either 60 Level 5 (diploma level) or 60 Level 6 (degree level) credits, through learning in the workplace. Candidates were selected on the basis of role responsibilities, academic profile and interest level.

When designing the programme, prime consideration was given to the rapidly changing nature of the working environment and role expectations of this group, all of whom were expected to lead the changes demanded of the government's agenda (all of the factors outlined above).

Furthermore they were all expected to support student nurses studying at diploma level, and some were expected to support community specialist practitioner students studying at degree level. It was therefore agreed that a scheme should be developed around the knowledge and competencies needed to deliver a modern service based on health need. Because many of these requirements are addressed through specialist practitioner preparation, the UKCC standards and competencies for specialist education and practice were pivotal to the development (UKCC, 1994, 1998). Furthermore, they arguably matched those areas of learning needed to meet the demands of the modernisation agenda. Another key element of the scheme was its relationship to practice. It was essential that all learning was relevant to practice and could benefit practice.

It was suggested that the time scale for three 20-credit themes would normally be in the region of 12–18 months. This was however flexible, depending on the individuals progress and circumstances. A detailed proposal which included the rationale for the development, stages to the process, an outline timetable, notional student workload, staff workload and assessment details was developed and submitted to the University's Quality Committee for approval. We commenced delivery in June 2001.

The Process

The process involved four phases, each of which encouraged the practitioner to adopt a systematic process to develop an area of practice which could be assessed and awarded academic credits.

The first stage was the profiling of practitioners to identify personal and professional achievement and to determine the level of study (diploma or degree). This involved practitioners providing details of all recordable and registrable qualifications as well as any accredited learning. These details were entered into a profiling document, all entries being checked against the original documents or written proof. On completion of the profiling exercise, practitioners were requested to reflect on their individual profile in the context of their current role and responsibilities, identifying any gaps in their knowledge and skills. They were given the competencies of community specialist practice as defined by the UKCC (1994, 1998) as a reference point. This was the starting point of their AWBL programme. The profiles were then collected and reviewed by the academic staff and the level of study confirmed in writing. At this stage progress files were commenced for each practitioner.

The second stage involved the selection of a topic area that had to be justified through reflecting on gaps in their own knowledge and practice. Practitioners achieved this in a number of ways, which included:

- The use of critical incidents drawn from practice
- Reference to the practice profile and health needs of the population
- The identification of gaps in service provision
- Reflecting on the priorities of the primary health care team and the primary care trust
- Locating the topic in the context of government policy.

The practitioners had to demonstrate that through exploration of the topic area they would be developing new skills and areas of knowledge relevant to contemporary practice, which could be mapped against the competencies of specialist practice.

Our rationale for using this bottom-up approach was twofold. First of all, we wanted to ensure the relevance of learning to practice, avoiding the 'technical rationality' mode described by Schon (1987). In doing so we were hoping to overcome the concern expressed by the Trust in relation to some courses having little relevance or benefit to practice. Secondly, this approach helps illuminate the complexity of professional practice, where the problems faced by professionals rarely have simple solutions. The starting point was therefore the learning that needed to take place to understand/solve the problems/develop an area of practice, allowing the practitioner to explore different forms of knowledge underpinning practice in greater depth, and further develop the skills necessary to deliver a quality service. In doing so we were drawing on the principles of reflection and enquiry based learning.

The topic areas selected by the first cohort of practitioners were varied and included:

- Promoting mother-infant interaction through massage
- Diabetic foot care – an educational package
- Developing a family health needs assessment tool for use within an orthodox Jewish community
- The role of the specialist practitioner as an educator
- Developing integrated care pathways for children with autism
- Establishing a therapeutic model of intervention in a Sure Start programme
- Promoting partnership working in health and social care.

However, these potentially huge topic areas had to be managed so that the learning was made explicit for assessment purposes. This was done through selecting three themes from the overall topic area. Each of the three themes had to be justified in the context of the overall topic as well as their relationship to each other. The student then had to identify four learning outcomes for each theme, together with a detailed action plan and indication of the evidence that would be supplied to demonstrate that learning had taken place and that the learning outcomes had been met. It was also a requirement that the learning outcomes reflected the level of study and could be mapped against the competencies of specialist practice. A programme of learning activity, the notional student workload and the assessment guidelines and criteria were approved by the Faculty Quality Committee to ensure academic standards were being met. The programme of learning included lectures and workshops, peer review sessions, practice skills development, as well as directed and independent study.

The next stage involved the practitioner undertaking the work outlined in the action plan and gathering evidence to support learning and skills development. This was developed into a portfolio of learning. A variety of evidence was acceptable which included:

- Literature/research reviews
- Critiques of the literature/research and bullet points
- Minutes of meetings

- Lesson plans
- Evidence of skills development
- Evidence of communication
- Reflective accounts/diaries
- Critiques of courses attended and reflection on learning
- Notes on learning from 'experts'
- Evaluations
- Review of policies and protocols
- Statistical data with accompanying analysis.

The final stage involved the students reflecting on both the process and product of learning. The group had chosen to do this at the close of each theme with an overall reflection at the end of their work. The use of reflection helped them to clarify their new learning as well as areas for further development. The assessment of learning was through a portfolio; each theme being worth 20 academic credits. There were two parts to the assessment strategy. The first part was a formative assessment of the overall rationale for the topic area, the themes, the learning outcomes and the action plan. The second was a summative assessment of the annotated evidence, showing achievement of the learning outcomes and including reflective accounts.

Reflection on the process

The first challenge that we had to overcome was our own anxiety about a strategy that neither of us had any experience of using. Although we were convinced that work based learning was the way forward for these experienced community nurses, and that new ways of working by Higher Education Institutions had to be tried and tested, we remained apprehensive. As a result of this we initially spent considerable amounts of time meeting with our colleagues to learn from their experiences, discussing the programme with the primary care manager and clinical leaders (who were happy for us to pilot this with the first group) and reflecting on our journey. As we have progressed, our confidence in using the process has grown. Some of the positive changes we have witnessed among the student group and the impact of their learning on practice have helped this.

Although all of the practitioners selected for the pilot programme were confident in their own area of practice and had had many years of experience as either a qualified health visitor or district nurse, they all expressed anxiety and indeed fear of engaging with Higher Education (HE). Many of these anxieties were about their own ability to succeed and the level of support they could expect from us. Considerable assurance had to be given about our role in supporting them as well as other mechanisms they could use, e.g. managers, mentors, experts in practice, staff from the Study Skills Centre at Northumbria University and library support. However, a year into the programme the group was unanimous in that one of the most valuable mechanisms for support was the peer review sessions that were structured into the timetable. The critical debate that emerged between the health visitors and district nurses, and the value they placed on each other's area of expertise demonstrated to us the potential for using this approach in a multi-professional arena. As with most learners the group expressed relief following feedback from the first summative assessment and since then have been much more relaxed about the process.

A further concern that they initially expressed was about the amount of time they would be allowed for study. Following a discussion involving the primary care manager it was agreed that because development aimed to improve their daily practice some of the work should be undertaken as part of their role as a specialist practitioner. In addition to this and timetabled sessions with us, four hours per month was allocated. Once the group embarked on the process this no longer became an issue.

A potential challenge for us was the vast array of topics selected by the practitioners. This did however prove manageable because of the small number in the group. We found that the use of reflective strategies and enquiry based approaches to learning were of value because not only did the group develop knowledge and skills in reflection and critical analysis, they provided a useful tool for challenging and questioning practice. The small group setting seemed to provide a safe environment where ideas could be shared, opinions listened to and valued, yet challenging questions could be posed without anyone feeling threatened, all factors which Brookfield (1987) suggests are crucial to the development of critical thinking.

Although the projects differed considerably in their focus, common areas of learning emerged. All the students successfully located their work in the policy context. Not only did they review a range of policies (national and local) to inform their rationale; they analysed these in terms of the implications for their role and function. Furthermore, every student presented evidence of why the development was needed in that specific practice population as well as within the organisation. In addition to this they all developed skills in information retrieval (many had never used IT systems before), critical appraisal, critical reflection, change management, practice development based on the 'best' available evidence, networking and partnership working, and evaluation. These areas can be mapped against many of the competencies of specialist practice (UKCC, 1994, 1998), and clearly relate to the skills and competencies needed to embrace the modernisation agenda. In addition to these areas of transferable knowledge and skills each practitioner researched and developed specific expertise depending on the topic selected. For example, a health visitor working in a Sure Start programme critically reviewed several therapeutic models of intervention, and visited other projects to see them in operation prior to selecting one to pilot in her own area of work. As part of this she attended a training course to develop her own skills in working with groups.

As we progressed through the programme we witnessed a dramatic change in all of the participants approach to learning and perhaps of more importance practice. This highly anxious group of experienced practitioners developed confidence in their own academic ability and expertise in practice. In their words they 'opened their eyes' to the real world of practice, challenging and questioning aspects of their own practice as well as that of others at a team and organisational level. Through their own reflections they suggest that they had been practicing sometimes in a traditional way, at others without real understanding of the why they had used a particular approach. Through developing the transferable skills gained through the AWBL they now feel confident and able to approach and deal with the many changes they are facing. The most rewarding part of the process for us is seeing them develop confidence in themselves and their enthusiasm towards practice development.

Conclusion

There is no doubt that community nurses will be judged against their ability to rise to and meet the challenges set out in the government's modernisation agenda. As providers of education we have a responsibility to work in partnership with our service colleagues to provide flexible education which prepares practitioners for their changing role in practice whilst at the same time meets the quality standards required of service and HE. For this to happen we need to feel supported when trying and testing new ways of working, reflecting on and continually developing the process. It was only through the encouragement of our colleagues from Gateshead Primary Care Trust and Northumbria University that we felt 'safe' to embark on this journey, enabling us to learn from the process. The encouragement and positive feedback that we have received from the practitioners themselves has convinced us that this strategy works. This has been reinforced through the comments of the external examiner and the primary care manager who has commissioned us to repeat the process with a second cohort of practitioners!

References

Audit Commission (2001) *Hidden Talents* (Audit Commission).

Bennett, J. (2002) *From Policy to Practice* in Canham. J. and Bennett, J. (eds) (2002) *Mentorship in Community Nursing: Challenges and Opportunities* (Blackwell Science, London).

Bennett, J. and Robinson, A. (2002) 'Developing Leadership Capacity in Community Nursing: the context of change.' *Journal of Community Nursing* 16 (12) pp. 4–5.

Bennett, J. and Robinson, A. (2003) 'Developing Leadership Capacity in Community Nursing: meeting the challenge.' *Journal of Community Nursing* 17 (1) pp. 22–24.

Birchenall, P. (1999) 'Developing a Work Based Learning philosophy.' *Nurse Education Today* (19) pp. 173–4.

Brennan, J. and Little, B. (1996) *A Review of Work Based Learning in Higher Education* (Open University Press, Milton Keynes).

Brookfield, S. (1987) *Developing Critical Thinkers* (Open University Press, Milton Keynes).

Canham, J. (2002) *Setting the Scene: Concepts of specialist practitioner and specialist practice* in Canham, J. and Bennett, J. (eds) (2002) *Mentorship in Community Nursing: Challenges and Opportunities* (Blackwell Science, London).

Department of Health (1997) *The New NHS, Modern, Dependable* (The Stationery Office. London).

Department of Health (1998) *A First Class Service: Quality in the New NHS* (DoH, Leeds).

Department of Health (1999a) *Making a Difference* (The Stationery Office, London).

Department of Health (1999b) *Saving Lives: Our Healthier Nation* (The Stationery Office, London).

Department of Health (2000a) *The NHS Plan* (The Stationery Office, London).

Department of Health (2000b) *A Health Service of all talents: developing the NHS workforce* (The Stationery Office, London).

Department of Health (2001) *Health inequalities: consultation on a plan for delivery* (The Stationery Office, London)

Department of Health (2002) *Working Together – Learning Together' A Framework for Lifelong Learning for the NHS* (The Stationery Office, London).

English National Board (1995) *Creating lifelong learners' guidelines for the implementation of the UKCC's Standards for Education and Practice following Registration* (ENB, London).

Ewan, C. and White, R. (1996) Teaching Nursing – A Self-instructional Handbook (2nd edn) (Chapman Hall, London).

Pritchard, P. and Pritchard, J. (1994) 'Teamwork for Primary and shared care.' *A Practical Workbook* (2nd edn) (Oxford Medical Publications, Oxford).

Schon, D. (1987) *Education the Reflective Practitioner* (Jossey-Bass, San Francisco).

Swallow, V., Chalmers, H. and Miller, J. (2000) 'Learning on the job Accredited Work Based Learning.' *Emergency Nurse* 8 (6).

Thompson, J.L. (1997) *Leading with Vision: Manage the Strategic Direction* (Thompson Business Press, London).

UKCC (1994) *Standards for Specialist Education and Practice* (UKCC, London).

UKCC (1998) *Standards for Specialist Education and Practice* (UKCC, London).

Part 2

The practitioner experience of Accredited Work Based Learning

Chapter 7

Emergency nurse practitioner role development through Accredited Work Based Learning

Julie Gillson and Mathew Brooksbank

According to the Department of Health (2001) there are too many people in NHS today who have to wait too long for the care and treatment they need. Reforming Emergency Care has been introduced as a substantive, proactive approach by the Government to guide and influence clearer pathways of care for patients attending A&E Departments.

Section 9.5 'Changes for Nurses' in *The NHS Plan* (DoH, 2000) states the new approach will shatter the old demarcations which have held back staff and slowed down care. NHS employers were required to empower appropriately qualified nurses to undertake a wider range of clinical tasks including the right to make and receive referrals, admit and discharge patients, order investigations and diagnostic tests, run clinics and prescribe drugs.

However, to fulfil this concept, Emergency Nurse Practitioner (ENP) roles have evolved nationally and now ENPs work as autonomous members of acute A&E teams in providing appropriate care and management for presenting patients. Previous demarcations of working practices have been highlighted and the role of the ENP examining patients with minor injuries has been adopted as an effective example of a new model of providing holistic care (DoH, 2001).

As discussed in Chapters 3 and 4, it was during the 1990s that Newcastle upon Tyne Hospitals NHS Trust recognised the importance and value of providing a structured development programme for experienced A&E nurses to practice autonomously. The concept of ENPs is not new, indeed in 1992 Burgoyn described an ENP as,

> '... *a nurse specialist who has a sound knowledge base in aspects of A&E nursing with additional preparation and skills in physical diagnosis, psychosocial assessment and prescribing of care and the preventative treatment'.*

Whilst examining the literature in this area it proved difficult to define the exact limitations of the ENP role. Throughout the country they appear to work at varying levels of practice, according to local needs and levels of training given (Bland, 1997; Sutton & Smith, 1995). Professional support is given by the Nursing and Midwifery Council (NMC) with their publication – *The Scope of Professional Practice* (updated 2000) and the Royal College of Nursing (RCN) who have produced guidelines and recommendations supporting ENP role developments (RCN, 1992). It also became evident that there is, to date, no nationally recognised qualification for nurses who complete ENP training and who practice at a local level (Cooper, 1996).

The ongoing Acute Services Review (ASR) in the Newcastle upon Tyne area resulted in the proposed improvement plan for Accident and Emergency services, however, academic clarification and recognition was paramount as an adjunct to providing ENPs with the credibility of being able to perform their role effectively. It was therefore recognised by the Head of Nursing that a collaboration with the Northumbria University should take place in order to accredit the learning. Discussion sessions and meetings took place with key stakeholders, which resulted in identifying the learning needs, objectives and criteria deemed essential by the nurses and medical staff, in order to make the transition to ENP. An AWBL programme incorporating six themes (Table 1, see p. 83) was established aiming to utilise the existing knowledge and skills possessed by experienced nurses involved, as well as anticipating and providing education and clinical instruction necessary in order to achieve competency in the development role. Depending on the individual's existing academic status, 60 academic credits could be achieved at either diploma level or degree level. To achieve these credits an assessment in three parts was a requirement:

1. Learning contract

2. Record of achievement

3. A reflective assignment.

Table I. Six themes, revolving around the concept of Emergency Nurse
Practitioner (ENP).

Clinical	Demonstrate within a systematic way, methods of assessment, diagnosis, treatment, management and care, within negotiated frameworks and protocols.
Theoretical	Consider the application of selected theoretical issues and concepts to practice events/incidents within the A&E environment.
Legal	Identify and critically appraise legal issues explicit and implicit within the role of emergency nurse practitioner in Accident and Emergency departments.
Communication and documentation	Establish effective and efficient communication systems and networks to enhance the role responsibilities of the emergency nurse in Accident and Emergency departments. Develop and appraise documentation systems for the safe collection and storage of data.
Professional boundaries	Identify and negotiate professional boundaries with other disciplines and establish parameter of role responsibilities.
Evaluation	Critically appraise self and systems within the context of the proposed emergency nurse role. Develop and critically appraise suitable audit mechanisms.

In this section the authors will describe their experiences as students on Cohort 1 (Julie) and Cohort 2 (Matthew) of AWBL

Role development

We are both experienced nurses with much common ground professionally. We both completed our nurse training in an era where traditionalism in nurse education was paramount, but both steered ourselves into the forefront of A&E nursing after qualifying as first level nurses. Our career pathways are similar in terms of having achieved successful promotion and undertaken further post registration qualifications including the Registered Sick Children's Nurse (RSCN) qualification and the English National Board (ENB 199) A&E qualification. Jointly our careers span approximately 30 years of working in an acute health care environment at the 'window of the hospital'.

We were each a member of either Cohort 1 or Cohort 2 of the AWBL programme. Although the structure and content of the educational experience for each cohort were the same, as individuals we experienced different problems and overcame separate difficulties before we completed the course. However, there were also common issues that provided us with material to use within our reflective diaries and as tools to aid our professional development.

Having been through a more traditional academic route, the flexible student-led theme of AWBL provided us with the first difficulty. Identifying our own learning outcomes initially proved problematic. As experienced senior nurses, verbalising then documenting one's shortfalls required self-examination to a level that we had not experienced for many years.

The AWBL process relied heavily upon, and frequently referred to the use of reflection in practice. Again traditional training had never called for formalisation of this, even though it has been performed subconsciously by every nurse, particularly following a critical incident.

After commencing the programme, we felt excited at the prospect of our future roles as ENPs. However, as the role developed, and we were able to reflect on the complexity of the work involved, particularly in terms of demonstrating learning and professional knowledge, we began to question our abilities, lacked confidence and felt very unsettled, even unhappy by the whole process. At this stage of the programme, we began to realise the true meaning of reflective practice, particularly after reading Kelly's (1994) statement,

> '... the importance of demonstrating learning through reflective practice should not be under-estimated.'

It seems pertinent to suggest that reflection should not just be a tool in which to improve one's practice, or as a measure of debriefing an incident where the outcome may have been better, but it should be used as a way of offering oneself praise, constructive criticism and above all evaluation and learning. Undertaking reflective practice enabled us to share information, grievances and knowledge with our colleagues in order to promote cognition and understanding.

Cohort 1 and 2 – Comparing and Contrasting

We outlined earlier in the text how we commenced the programme in two separate cohorts, and even though they ran concurrently, there was an obvious difference in how the selection process was achieved.

Awareness at a local level in the late 1990s of future imminent changes within emergency reform were at the forefront of every A&E nurse's mind. Periodicals and nursing press appeared to be giving more credence and information in relation to emergency nurses expanding their roles into the field of autonomy. This new approach had actually been highlighted within our unit, and a number of nurses, with eventual agreement from the medical staff, proactively explored the feasibility of nurses assessing minor injuries at triage. As early as 1996, a questionnaire was completed for each relevant patient by the triage nurse outlining whether or not, after taking a history, they would send the patient to x-ray. It was then compared at a later stage with the final outcome once the patient had been examined by the doctor. On reflection, the study was very informal, and although the results proved favourable for nurses – as it demonstrated they would have initiated more appropriate x-rays, we are aware that there were gaps within the data and on critical analysis a truly comparative result was not possible.

It is an irony that less than two years later in reaction to the forthcoming reforms in emergency care, senior nurses were strongly encouraged to take an active part in the involvement of the role of ENP. The nurses involved took up this challenge robustly with optimism and enthusiasm yet coupled with uncertainty and fear of the unknown.

Cohort 1 were involved at the conception of the initial negotiations with the Trust and the University. The strategic planning stage involved outlining role descriptions, the evolvement of patient group directives and most importantly issues such as vicarious liability. The Programme Management Group (PMG) gave good strategic direction in forming a successful collaboration between all professional bodies involved. Once all parties were in agreement with the learning package developed, Cohort 1 began their training.

Cohort 1 – Julie Gillson

In 1998, at the onset of this development I was practising as a G grade Sister of approximately 11 years standing within A&E. I had been aware of the evolution of ENP's nationally and was keen to introduce this development into the department in which I was working. I felt confident to take on the challenge of this role, as I felt I had been performing several aspects of the new role in an advisory capacity to junior doctors for many years.

I was approached at the very early stages and took an active role in the developmental stages of the AWBL programme. I felt this move forward was essential for both individual professional development and to improve the service delivery to patients attending A&E.

Myself and 11 other established sisters at both F and G grades, made up the first cohort and due to internal pressures such as the acute service review, previously mentioned, had a target date of February 2000 to be 'up and running' as competent ENPs. A great deal of work was carried out behind the scenes to encourage senior medical staff from other specialities to become part of the training process and eventually protocols and a training plan were agreed upon and the serious business of learning could begin.

At the onset of our training we had approximately eight months to attend lectures, have supervised practise and produce academic work to support our achievements. Due to the high level of support from our Head of Nursing, appropriate time out was given in the clinical field to allow supervision from medical staff as we navigated our way into our new role. Northumbria University provided academic support by identifying supervisors who had been involved with the development of the ENP role from the beginning. They were aware of the problems and pitfalls already overcome and therefore were able to provide a dynamic and flexible approach to allow nurses to achieve their full potential.

Direct clinical support was afforded by a General Practitioner who had, for a year, been working full-time within A&E. The employment of this doctor had come about as a result of another Trust initiative to improve services offered to patients attending the department. As many patients who presented to A&E did so with a predominately primary care problem employing a GP with an interest in emergency care, had proved successful at not only reducing the waiting times for these patients, but also freeing up more time for A&E doctors to see urgent cases more quickly.

The academic side of this programme proved problematic in the initial stages, the learning contract was a new concept to myself and most of my colleagues. I was unfamiliar with such a learning tool and I was unsure and anxious about what was expected from me. It took many weeks and numerous visits to my academic supervisor before I was able to logically structure my individual learning requirements. At this stage, I began to have my first doubts about my ability to complete the programme.

These feelings heightened when I began to contemplate my assignment. The main focus of this piece of work was to use reflection to demonstrate the learning process and to record and reflect upon critical incidences. I had heard of reflection in practice but to my knowledge I did not use it and felt that reflection was yet another 'buzz' word from the academic world. As I researched the use of reflection and examined the literature available, I was surprised to discover that I did use reflection in my working practises albeit in an ad hoc fashion, however, I still had some difficulty in expressing the process of reflection in the written work I was required to complete.

The last academic hurdle was how our competencies were to be assessed. It had been agreed that to prove credibility with our medical colleagues our clinical skills should be assessed using a tried and trusted medical assessment tool, that of Objective Structured Clinical Examination (OSCE). The scope of our practice was to be limited to injuries, elbow and below, knee and below and included lacerations, burns and scalds as well as common orthopaedic injuries. For each area there was to be an individual OSCE and all assessments had to be passed before being able to practice more autonomously.

My only experience of OSCE had been to listen to horrifying tales from junior doctors that had been grilled by ageing consultants in darkened rooms for hours on end. As a group we were so concerned about this process that we collectively requested an alternative method of assessment. After great discussion and much reassurance from one of our consultants, we agreed on a modified OSCE that would involve a seen assessment tool that we could work up to before our actual examination.

Our clinical supervisor developed this and she was to be our named assessor. This alleviated some of our fears, however, I still found the process intimidating.

Lectures were programmed throughout the eight months and were delivered by participating consultants from the specialities directly involved or affected by the introduction of ENPs in addition to University staff and experts such as a solicitor. The formal sessions were held within Trust accommodation and even though this time out was not protected, attendance was high. These lectures proved useful to both parties involved, they were of a high but understandable level and many of the consultants involved had opportunity to experience our increasing knowledge base and confidence.

As our knowledge base increased we stepped up our clinical supervision within the A&E department. Protected time out was incorporated into the staffing levels and we had the luxury of shadowing the medical staff while they examined patients. This was extremely important as I realised that I needed to change my approach to patients and their presenting condition and I would need to use a more structured medical model if I was to obtain the information required to provide the patient with the care and treatment they needed.

Full explanations were given to patients involved in our training and verbal consent was obtained before they took part. In my experience no patient refused to be involved and the common consensus was that they were more than happy with the prospect of nurses providing them with the treatment plan they required.

During our clinical supervision we decided as a group not to wear our uniforms but to wear everyday clothing and our identity badge. The reasoning behind this was twofold, firstly it gave a message to our colleagues that we were not on the 'shop floor' thus protecting our time from the pressures of work within the department. Secondly, it seemed to put us in a different mind set, giving us the confidence to take on our new role.

During the eight months that led up to the introduction of ENPs, there were many highs and many more lows. Other internal changes were putting pressure on senior staff and often we thought that we would never achieve our goal. We lost three members of the first cohort when the Government introduced the 'NHS Direct' scheme, whether this was solely due to the pressures of the AWBL programme is debatable but I am sure it played a minor part in the resignation of some of the staff involved.

As we moved through our training programme, the second cohort began their course. Changes had been introduced into their programme, many due to our experiences and we were able to support and encourage our colleagues to achieve their full potential.

Cohort 2 – Matthew Brooksbank

In April 1999, I returned to the A&E Department after successfully completing my Registered Nurse Diploma in Children's Nursing (RNCh Dip HE). My Senior Nurse Manager approached me soon after my return and asked me if I would like to commence the AWBL programme scheduled for commencement in May of that year. At this time, I was an E grade Staff Nurse with a wealth of A&E experience, however, I questioned why I had been selected to commence the ENP training programme, as I was led to believe, at this stage, it was only available to F and G grade nurses. I was informed that directives from the Head of Nursing had called for dually qualified nurses to be included in the training programme. This included myself and two other nurses of the same grade. There was an air of bad feeling initially to the three of us from other colleagues who were of the same grade and level of experience, one of them being my best friend. We found that we had to 'ride the storm' for a short while – but like most things, tensions and aggressions waned, and eventually they became very supportive of us.

A meeting was called for myself and six other colleagues to discuss the training programme. This was held at another hospital in the area, because unlike Cohort 1, Cohort 2 commenced training in collaboration with A&E nurses from another local trust. Members of the group consisted of academic tutors, A&E Consultants and Senior Nurses from both hospitals and nurses assigned for training from both hospitals. As with colleagues in Cohort 1, the meeting outlined strategies connected with the ENP training – emphasising the importance of creating a negotiated learning contract to support the AWBL. The learning contract encapsulated the six themes revolving around the concept of the ENP as illustrated in Table 1.

In contrast to Cohort 1, at the meeting each prospective ENP trainee was issued with a full timetable for the work based learning course. The commencement date was the 21 May 1999 and completion date 3 November 1999 with a hand-in date for the reflective essay on 7 January 2000. The timetable outlined lectures and venues and included amongst others, anatomy and physiology, radiology and legal issues. We were also allocated 12 four hour periods of clinical shadowing, clearly documented in the timetable.

The lectures commenced several weeks after the meeting, allowing us all a little time to familiarise ourselves with the documentation and give some thought to the negotiated learning contract. It appears that the same dilemma encountered by our colleagues in Cohort 1, also faced us too. As a collective group, one of our main anxieties expressed in informal discussions was in relation to the learning contract, in particular trying to understand the 'academic tone and language'. This appeared to be the first of our many forthcoming crises – generally feeling that if we can't understand the articulated requirements – how were we going to progress into the realms of autonomy. On a personal note, I, like my co-author, had to arrange a number of meetings with my academic tutor, before I could express what exactly my learning needs would be.

I had just completed a diploma course, and foolishly believed myself to be 'well read', but the prospect of pitching my learning and academic abilities at a level higher, and after reading the 'explanatory notes' of the learning contract, left me with a belief that the only form of literature I would feel comfortable in understanding would be nothing more taxing than a copy of the '*Beano*'. I recall a short period of 'trying to forget' my learning contract existed and found a new home for it in the corner of my front room, concealed by a chair. This procrastination went on for over two weeks, however, I remember thinking that I was spending so much time worrying about the fact that I hadn't began to think about my learning needs, using so much negative energy in doing so, that one afternoon I sat quietly, resurrected the carrier bag full of paper from behind the chair, and simply listed what I wanted to get out of the course, what I wanted to learn, how I conceived I was realistically going to learn it, and the inner anxieties I had about learning. I then made an appointment with my academic tutor who offered support in breaking down each section in order to document it with the appropriate academic parlance. This appeared to be the first turning point, offering a ray of sunshine, opening my road to a more focused horizon.

After this initial anxiety had been somewhat allayed, the second problem loomed. My work rota had been drawn up to include several weeks of night duty due to staffing sickness and unfilled vacancies (due to the birth of NHS Direct). Lectures were due to start, and I found that I was working night shift. This meant having to get up early in the afternoons to attend my lectures, often spending long periods of time in heavy traffic, hence adding more time to the day when I should have been in bed. The prospect of three weeks nights did not in effect seem too bad, but this three weeks finally became seven months, and due to the forthcoming changes in Newcastle in relation to A&E services, the shifts were busy with massive influxes of patients. These were without doubt the busiest and most emotionally and physically trying period of night duties I had ever encountered in my A&E career.

I consider myself very lucky in terms of my choice of a clinical preceptor. I chose a very experienced Sister for whom I already had great respect as an A&E nurse, and furthermore, a professional who I still try to emulate in my own practice. She was a member of Cohort 1, and her guidance and reflection helped me to recognise the responsibilities linked to the ENP role, and raised my awareness to practice and how much of a resource I could become to my patients. We both share much common beliefs with regard to patient care. We both believe in maintaining high standard of care, I recall her instilling in me the need to remember my origins and although a new role was beckoning – never to lose sight of maintaining the caring element of my practice. Working alongside my preceptor enabled me to discuss areas of the AWBL programme and become more '*au fait*' with them. She helped me forge my understanding of the concepts and made the relationship of academia to clinical practice more clear. At no time did she make me feel inferior as she herself had already encountered these anxieties and had reflected on them.

The long period of night duty did, however, interfere greatly with aspects of clinical shadowing. It was impossible to obtain this on nights, where the only doctors available were Senior House Officers (SHOs), they themselves not greatly experienced clinicians. I did attend most of the planned clinical shadowing sessions with the consultants and registrars, however at times these were not always beneficial. The amount of learning I was able to achieve was dependent on which senior doctor was holding the clinic and also on the numbers of patients attending. Some of the doctors were very keen to explain and allow some hands-on clinical examination, whereas others appeared to be paying more 'lip service' to our development.

There was also great competition from other colleagues to attend the shadowing sessions, so this in turn also affected learning outcomes and developments.

Although, over the course of seven months on night duty, I had been able to clinically examine many patients; I was consciously aware that I had not undertaken any of my assessments in order to be deemed competent to practice autonomously. I approached my Senior Nurse and expressed my concerns. She was very supportive and suggested I return to day duty and spend several weeks working solely within the newly opened Minor Injuries Unit (MIU) at the Royal Victoria Infirmary (RVI). I remember feeling very anxious at this stage, because all my colleagues had completed most of their assessments. I felt as though I was wading in a pool of quicksand and lagging greatly behind.

The move to the MIU was the complement to my development that I undoubtedly needed. As it had just opened, support was given to the Nurse Practitioners by two doctors. They both worked one week on and one week off, always opposite to each other. One was a Middle Grade who had worked within the realms of A&E for many years, the other, a GP who also had a wealth of A&E experience. My arrival at the MIU came just at the right time. The department had just opened and was relatively quiet, allowing for the Middle Grade to spend a lot of time discussing and demonstrating elements of clinical practice. On reflection, I believe I learned more about the whole ethos of autonomy in these two weeks than in the overall length of the course. I could feel my confidence building after every patient I examined. At last I felt comfortable with the thought of my new role. I comfortably passed my assessments within this valuable two-week period.

In February 2000, I was working as an autonomous practitioner at both the MIU and at the WIC at Newcastle General Hospital.

It seems ironic, that for a person, who despite a yearning to learn and develop, had so many reservations about undertaking a new role, I now work solely as an ENP and can place my hand on my heart and honestly say that I have finally found my true niche within my professional life.

Conclusion

The evolved role of the ENP in Newcastle is a prime example of practice in action attributed to the elements of AWBL. Due to the successful collaboration of the University and Hospital Trust, the city of Newcastle now offers additional and effective complementary services on two main hospital sites to patients with minor injuries and minor ailments. Both the Minor Injuries Unit at the RVI and the Walk-in Centre at Newcastle General Hospital have, over the past two and a half years, became well known and well respected with the general public. Numbers of attendees have doubled in this time through word of mouth from satisfied patients using the service offered to them by autonomous nurse practitioner. Training and development successfully continues to new cohorts of nurses using the AWBL approach, even though some elements have been refined since earlier cohorts engaged on the programme.

It appears that through the application of AWBL, other indirect learning facets have developed, challenging nurses to look at their future practice from different dimensions. As two individuals from the programme, we now understand and appreciate aspects of importance such as change innovation, risk and ethical issues and in particular taking 'ownership' for our practice. AWBL is a flexible but robust form of academic support to clinical expertise. Moreover, it allows for diversity in the changing of roles – for example, as two practitioners, we initially commenced the programme as Senior Nurses engaged in doing the same role, however, now one of us specialises as a Paediatric Emergency Nurse Practitioner and the other works as an Emergency/Primary Care Practitioner with an interest in conducting a men's health clinic.

Academically, AWBL has allowed us to branch into further aspects of learning, giving confidence to approaching lifelong learning with a critical way of thinking and challenging old assumptions and beliefs. Completing the AWBL process we have both chosen to specialise in different areas as follows:

Julie is now working 30 hours per week as a paediatric nurse practitioner within the A&E department, focusing on children whom attend with minor injuries and some minor ailments. A development programme is being considered by the A&E department to expand this role in to more complicated medical problems using protocols and guidelines already in use by SHOs. With the introduction of a part-time paediatric specialist registrar in the A&E department specialist training will be readily available and consideration is been given to using an AWBL programme so that more ENPs could advance their training and become Paediatric Emergency Nurse Practitioners (PENPs). For the remaining seven-and-a-half hours Julie is an Honorary Research Associate at Northumbria University for one year looking at the impact of AWBL on the developing role of ENPs in A&E within Newcastle Hospitals. This study has actively involved the key stake-holders involved with the training of ENPs and has put down foundation stones of future developments and advances for ENPs as well as creating research opportunities within the A&E service. Julie has recently qualified as an advanced nurse prescriber and is also about to commence an MA in autonomous practice within Northumbria University once again using AWBL.

Mathew is working full-time as a Primary/Emergency Nurse Practitioner within the Walk-in Centre (WIC) in Newcastle. This WIC was one of the first set-up by the Government in February 2000 and is able to provide patients with an extensive service for minor injuries and minor ailments. Nurse practitioners have access to x-ray, laboratory facilities and referral pathways through the secondary care systems as well as direct links to GPs and other primary care services. To date, Mathew is in the process of developing a 'well man' service. A pilot clinic was run providing patients with a full range of advice and investigations and due to its success further sponsorship has been obtained and Matthew intends to provide a regular service to men within the Newcastle region. Academically, Mathew is registered for an MA (Advanced Practice) and is presently studying to become an advanced nurse prescriber.

It is at this juncture, that we are now able to truly reflect on our experiences. At times it has been unclear, even traumatic, but with the ongoing support of academics we now feel that accreditation to compliment ones practice does help formalise the authenticity of ones clinical role.

> *'Accredited Work Based Learning is a method of learning and assessment which is pivotal to new nursing roles. Through AWBL, A&E nurses have been able to develop their practice, derive learning from experience and gain accreditation at a level appropriate to their academic status'.* (Swallow *et al.* 2000)

This statement encapsulates the whole ethics and philosophy of AWBL in conjunction with adding the final 'spit and polish' to achieve sound clinical autonomous practice.

Reflection

One of the main requirements of the AWBL programme was for each ENP trainee to submit a reflective essay at the end of the course, detailing their feelings and using critical incidents to support reflection in practice. Without doubt, reflection is something that is personal – taking into account feelings, problem-solving skills and decision-making. Atkins and Murphy (1993) suggest that in order to be a reflective practitioner it is necessary to develop skills of self-awareness, description, critical analysis, synthesis and evaluation.

At the beginning of the programme, our academic supervisors instilled in us the need to reflect. At this stage we all felt as though we were 'novices', as many of us had not previously used reflection in theoretical work during our traditional training. We were advised and channelled to use one model of reflection which best suited our learning needs and feelings at the time.

There are a number of models of reflection available aimed to assist a professional to understand and utilise a reflective approach to practice. Gibbs (1998) describes 'the Reflective Cycle' which works through six phases (Figure 1). This model enables critical analysis of incidents and practice in a logical sequence to both individuals and groups alike. Bouds's (1985) Model of Reflection places emphasis on individuals feelings stating that *'only after feelings have been dealt with, should an event be analysed and evaluated'* (Figure 2) – Benner's (1984) Novice to Expert Model of Reflection describes the wealth of untapped knowledge encapsulated in clinical practice and the knowledge of expert clinicians. She suggests that to encourage the expansion of knowledge and development, nurses need to systematically record what they learn through experience, suggesting that *'... if learning is to occur from practice, then reflection is vital'.*

Figure 1. The Reflective Cycle (Gibbs, 1988).

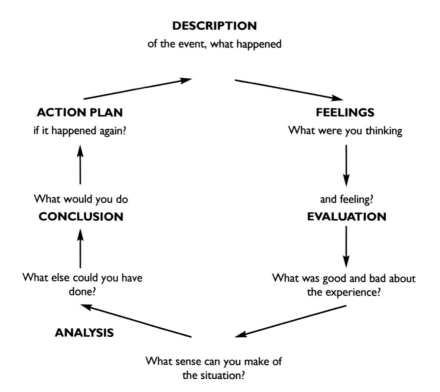

DESCRIPTION
of the event, what happened

ACTION PLAN
if it happened again?

FEELINGS
What were you thinking

What would you do
CONCLUSION

and feeling?
EVALUATION

What else could you have
done?

What was good and bad about
the experience?

ANALYSIS

What sense can you make of
the situation?

Figure 2. Boud's Model of Reflection (1985).

EXPERIENCE	REFLECTIVE PROCESS	OUTCOMES
Behaviour	Returning to experience	New perspectives
Ideas	Attending to feelings	Changes in behaviour
Feelings	Positive / Negative	Readiness to act
	Re-evaluating experiences	

Individual cohorts, at times found it difficult to base their entire learning development by simply relating it to one reflective model. The general consensus of opinion from all of us was that each model was relevant to us in different ways and at different stages of our learning pathway. However, if a choice was to be made, in relation to the efficacy of a certain model, the majority of us as ENP trainees tended to gravitate towards the works of Benner. We were all experienced in our clinical practice – many of us considering ourselves expert, but with the birth of a new role – the expert within us became very much the novice once more. This was demonstrated in our critical incidents documented in our reflective diaries. Individual examples of which are as follows:

Incident 1 (Cohort 1)

An early anxiety for me was to prove to my medical colleagues that I was able to perform the role of ENP. I had for many years advised junior doctors on how patients should be treated and now I had to demonstrate that my knowledge had a sound basis. I felt I was viewed by both nursing and medical staff as experienced in my field of work as a so-called expert and I now had the opportunity to prove it.

I began my clinical placements discussing with my medical supervisor my learning needs and requirements. We decided that I would examine patients without the doctor being present, document my findings then accompany the doctor on their examination.

After three patients had been examined, I began to feel uncomfortable. Although my initial diagnosis and planned treatment were not grossly incorrect, they were not wholly appropriate or correctly documented in comparison to the doctor's findings. My confidence began to wane and I became withdrawn and lacked enthusiasm, even avoiding opportunities to examine patients who fell within my remit.

I had tried to prove my skills before I had learnt them; I was trying to conceal my worries and feelings of inadequacy by attempting to become proficient without the training. This attitude had also been compounded by senior medical colleagues who had made comments such as:

'You've been doing it for years, it won't be a problem, or its easy, don't worry.'

Statements that had not allowed me to become the student. Their attitude implied I was still the expert, whereas in reality, I was the novice and I had only just had the courage to recognise this. I admitted to my medical supervisor that we needed to change our strategy and that she needed to start at the beginning, talking me through the basics of examination techniques and of history taking.

From then on I allowed myself to be the novice and with encouragement and support started to move towards expert.

Incident 2 (Cohort 2)

I had been working alongside my medical supervisor on one of my clinical shadowing days. I explained to him that I particularly liked lacerations because of the challenging aspect of 'making a silk purse out of a pigs ear' in relation to ragged, untidy lacerations. In my previous A&E employment, I had attained an expanded role in suturing, and regularly sutured many types of wounds. On this particular day, my supervisor and I had been discussing my learning contract in relation to finger injuries when a patient presented with a laceration to his finger.

After taking a clinical history with my medical supervisor in attendance, we learned that the patient worked as a refuse collector, and whilst cleaning away some abandoned rubbish bags, he sustained a deep laceration over the dorsum of his finger at the proximal inter-phalangeal joint. I was happy with the examination I had done, paying particular attention to extensor tendon function and neur-ovascular status. I concluded by relaying my management plan to my medical supervisor. I planned to perform a soft tissue x-ray to rule out any glass foreign body and then perform wound closure by suture due to the location of the laceration.

My supervisor commended me on my examination but suggested that I would need to fully assess that there had been no joint capsule disruption prior to closure. With this comment, I did not know whether I had taken one step forward or two steps back. I questioned my own ability and then had pangs of anxiety, believing that my examination was insufficient. I realised that I had approached this particular patient with too much confidence. I believed that just because I had prior knowledge and experience of suturing wounds that I foolishly believed that wound closure was the only requirement. I discussed this at length with my supervisor, who was extremely supportive, but despite this did not help with my crisis of confidence. It has been documented earlier in the chapter the importance of reflection and the models preferred by most of us, i.e. Benner (1984). However on this occasion, I felt that my feelings related more to Schon's (1992) description of being in 'swampy lowlands' where problems are often 'confusing and hard to control'. This occasion gave me the true realisation of being a novice – a role initially difficult to accept after being perceived by my colleagues, and to some degree my own self-perception in my previous role as being an expert. This was truly a learning experience through reflective practice.

References

Atkins, S. and Murphy, K. (1993) 'Reflection: a review of the literature.' *Journal of Advanced Nursing* 18 (8) pp. 1, 188–92.

Bland, A. (1997) 'Developing the Emergency Nurse Practitioners role in Accident & Emergency 'a bottom-up approach.' *A&E Nursing* (5) pp. 42–47.

Bouds, D., Keogh, R. and Walker, D. (1985) 'Reflection: a review of the literature.' *Journal of Advanced Nursing* 18(4) pp. 1,188–1,192.

Bugoyne, S. (1992) 'Emergency Nurse Practitioner.' *Nursing Standard* (6.2) pp. 12.

Cooper, M. (1996) 'Nurse practitioners in A&E – a literature review.' *Emergency Nurse* (4) pp. 19–22.

Department of Health (2000) *The NHS Plan: a plan for investment, a plan for reform* (The Stationery Office, London).

Department of Health (2001) *Reforming Emergency Care* (DoH, London).

Gibbs, G. (1988). *Learning by doing: a guide to teaching and learning methods* (EMU Oxford University, Oxford).

Kelly, J. (1994) 'On Reflection.' *Practice Nurse* (1–14) pp. 188–190.

RCN (1992) *Emergency Nurse Practitioners guidance from the Royal College of Nursing* (RCN Accident and Emergency Association, London).

Schon, D. (1992) *The Reflective Practitioner* (Jossey-Bass, California).

Sutton, F. and Smith, C. (1995) 'Advanced nursing practice: new ideas and new perspectives.' *Journal of Advanced Nursing* (21) pp. 1,073–1,043.

Swallow, V., Chalmers, H. and Miller, J. (2000) 'Learning on the job: Accredited Work Based Learning for nurses.' *Emergency Nurse* 8(6) pp. 35–38.

United Kingdom Central Council (2000) *The Scope of Professional Practice* (UKCC, London).

Chapter 8

Reflection in Accredited Work Based Learning for personal development

Sarah Wimpenny

Introduction

As one of the first cohort of students at Northumbria to undertake the BA (Hons) Nursing Practice degree I was supported to apply for 60 credits towards my degree through AWBL. This was a new style of learning for me which involved:

- Identification of three themes relating to my practice
- Development of four personal learning outcomes relating to each theme
- Achievement of the learning outcomes
- Submission of:
  - a portfolio of evidence of achievement of my learning outcomes supported by reflective annotations of my learning while gathering the evidence.
  - a 4000-word critical and reflective account of an aspect of my learning during the AWBL process.

We embarked on the six-month AWBL process in May 2000 and attended initial workshops at the University during which the process was explained. We were each allocated an academic mentor and identified a clinical colleague from our practice setting to act as clinical mentor. Within this partnership we were each supported to develop a tripartite learning contract in which we identified our three themes, personal learning outcomes and an agreed action plan for achieving the learning outcomes.

After a lot of thought and discussion with my mentors I identified the following three themes:

- Teaching and assessing in practice
- Managing change in the workplace
- Evidence based practice.

Each of my themes is under-pinned by one essential factor. That factor is education of practitioners in the workplace. These were all issues that I had previously explored while studying for the English National Board courses (ENB 100 and 998) and the Diploma in Higher Education (Nursing Science). Therefore, I saw this new learning experience as an opportunity to explore these issues in more depth, to see something tangible happening in the workplace as a result of my learning and to ultimately gain credit towards my degree.

In this chapter I will explore and discuss aspects of my own learning that occurred during the AWBL process, in particular relating to two of my learning outcomes which were:

- To demonstrate an ability to influence Practitioners' educational development within the Critical Care area.
- To explore and discuss alternative routes to Practitioners' professional development in Critical Care.

The AWBL experience gave me the opportunity to explore how my own personal and professional development has evolved since my career began in the Intensive Care Unit (ITU), back in 1993. I was able to examine my experience of education on the previously mentioned courses and consider how this has influenced the way I now approach my responsibility for Practitioners' educational and professional development.

To illustrate my own learning during the AWBL I will consider how the AWBL process allowed me to develop and refine my own critical and analytical skills and how my own learning during the process has led me to visualise the way education and the nurse's role could progress within the Critical Care environment. In this way I hope to explain how I have come to 'learn about my own learning' while becoming increasingly responsible for facilitating the learning of others in the workplace.

Reflection on practice in Critical Care

The Audit Commission (1999) and the DoH (2000) explored the provision of critical care services and their recommendations included that:

- more high dependency beds should be made available by the NHS.

- we should adopt more flexible ways of working and workforce planning, which could enable us to deliver a more cost effective service in the Critical Care area.

At the time of writing I am currently a G grade sister in charge of a brand new High Dependency Unit (HDU) which is one of a number of Critical Care areas within the Newcastle upon Tyne Hospitals NHS Trust. Part of my responsibility is to support the educational and professional development of the staff with whom I work and develop protocols and guidelines for nurses to use in what is a relatively new area of critical care. To do this I need to use every aspect of my change management skills. Since qualifying as a Registered General Nurse (RGN) I have always striven to continue my professional development, by undertaking various courses and attending study days. The opening of the new HDU has meant that I have had to work very hard to enable boundaries between traditional Critical Care units and HDU to be broken down. The process is on going.

It is only through learning to use reflection as a tool to explore my own learning during the AWBL process (Johns, 1995) and as I have matured into a management role, that I have come to realise what I have gained from my earlier educational experience. I have learned to reflect 'on' as well as 'in' action (Schon 1987). Therefore, I would like to share with colleagues some of my insight into my own learning in the hope that they will learn to value their own on-going learning much sooner than I did.

I completed the ENB 100 when I was a D grade Staff Nurse and in a unit with a very hierarchical culture. As part of the course I produced a protocol for use when delivering eye care to patients in the unit. In developing this I was successful in gaining support and guidance from a Consultant Ophthalmologist. The protocol was subsequently adopted for use in the unit, which, given my junior status at the time was an achievement in its own right. As the literature suggests, for change to take place it is important for the agent to have the necessary skills for implementation. Mauksch and Miller (1981) say they should have commitment to the change, be competent in nursing knowledge, nursing practice and interpersonal relationships and communication skills. The status of the change agent has a lot of influence in successful implementation of change, (Lancaster & Lancaster, 1982; Bowman, 1986; Tross & Cavanagh, 1996; Morison, 1992; Haynes, 1992). I now realise that because I had persuaded the

Consultant Ophthalmologist to become involved in the protocol development this gave the protocol added credibility; having someone to champion the cause is a strategy strongly recommended in the literature (Smith, Galinest & Manthey, 1995).

After producing the protocol I gave little thought to how this achievement was a sign of my own personal and professional growth. However, through analysing my achievement in relation to my AWBL learning outcomes, I realised that developing this protocol had been a valuable learning experience for me. It had provided me with the opportunity to retrospectively explore my own professional development. Having to think back five years to the process involved and considering the stage of professional development I was at when I devised the protocol made me realise that I had intuitively used skills of change management. There is no doubt that at the time I had no concept of the processes of change, very few networking skills and limited computer skills.

On reflection, I saw the work as very low-key. My analysis of the nursing knowledge within the unit at that time in preparation for the protocol development was very small-scale. This is recognised as a problem with nursing research as nurses have a tendency to engage in one-off studies in areas of interest to them and often use small sample sizes in research (Close & Cheater, 1999), so begging the question, how reliable is the evidence produced by these projects and should they be used to base practice on?

Since completing the ENB 998, my interest in teaching has spiraled. At the time I hated formal teaching and would do anything to avoid it. The thought of standing up in front of people and teaching or presenting something 'left me cold'. However, through reminding myself to teach and using the skills gained during the ENB 998, I have become more confident. I have found that with good preparation and a sound knowledge of the topic, as advocated in the literature (Wragg, 1994; Kember *et al.* 2001) the experience of sharing knowledge with others can be very fulfilling.

In 1998, I was appointed to the post of Acting F grade staff nurse in the Trust. This role included responsibility for supporting the ITU staff in a neighbouring hospital with the relocation of burns and plastics patients to another unit. Using a reflective approach within one of my learning outcomes for AWBL gave me the opportunity to explore just how much of a contribution I had made to the process of the specialty being moved to another unit. My colleagues were happy to fill in evaluations and testimonials demonstrating how my teaching sessions, and unit preparation for burns patients, greatly aided them in the care of such patients. This provided valuable authentic evidence to support the achievement of one of my learning outcomes.

In order to be effective in my current role, self-awareness is necessary. Burns (1982) and Hinchliff (1999) claim that how the teacher perceives themselves and others will affect their teaching ability. On analysing my own teaching skills I find that Wong's (1978) nine categories of helpful teaching behaviour summarises my approach well:

- Show a willingness to answer questions and offer explanations.
- Treat students with interest and respect.
- Uses encouragement and praise.
- Informs students of their progress.
- Has a pleasant voice.
- Is accessible to students.
- Supervisors effectively.
- Expresses confidence both in self and students.

These characteristics coupled with a keen interest in the subject, and the creation of an effective teaching environment (Wragg, 1994) have made me successful within this role and encouraged me to increase my input in the education of others. As an F grade sister my remit within the unit at that time was staff education. Over the two years in this post I was heavily involved in all aspects of my colleagues professional development. This involved organising twice-weekly teaching sessions on subjects of interest to nurses within Critical Care.

In addition I was asked to compile a database of nursing staff's professional qualifications, so that we have a record available for allocation of study leave and to ensure that enough people have the relevant qualifications such as the ENB 100. The Audit Commission (1999), recommended that a minimum of 25% of Critical Care nurses should possess the ENB 100 and that the ENB 998 or the City and Guilds 730 must be held by those mentoring students (since 2002 ENB courses have been replaced with other relevant programmes, however, the principle of appropriate preparation for a role remains).

My other area of responsibility was to organise in-house training, including new staff induction days, the development of structured preceptorship booklets and role expansion booklets. This is particularly important in my mind so as to ensure new staff get the best possible introduction to ITU. If newly qualified nurses are stressed through lack of support and education it has a direct affect on staff retention (Coad & Haines, 1999).

My vision of nurse education in the future

Whilst in my F grade position I developed guidelines for caring for patients on Continuous Positive Airway Pressure (CPAP), for the surgical special care area.

After discussing further training needs for staff with the ward sister, I provided a teaching package on invasive monitoring and did teaching sessions on subjects requested by the staff. Unfortunately I was not able to continue this educational link with the ward due to staffing pressures on their ward, leaving little time for staff development. I would have liked the opportunity to resume these links and further develop the educational input to wards.

Through exploration of my own learning during the AWBL I have come to the conclusion that increasing support for staff development in the HDU will benefit both staff and patients and help prevent some unnecessary re-admissions to Critical Care areas. This belief was supported by a number of authors (Gibson, 1997; Coad & Hines, 1999; Audit Commission, 1999; DoH, 2000). The latter document calls for the development of outreach services to be developed as an integral part of each NHS Trust's Critical Care service and suggest these will have three essential objectives:

- To avert admissions
- To enable discharges
- To share critical care skills.

Thankfully the Government recognised the pressures on Critical Care services and released extra money to make available an increased number of HDU beds at the end of 2000.

There is a huge ongoing need for educational development in Critical Care. Whilst senior nurses in Critical Care do a very good job in trying to meet the educational needs of staff on the unit I have felt for a long time that one way of improving the situation further would be the creation of posts such as Clinical Nurse Educators (CNEs) or Lecturer Practitioners (LP).

In 2000, two Northumbria posts were created as joint posts between the Trust and the University. These post-holders have had a great impact on nurse development in Critical Care, however, because they are joint posts, they also have academic responsibilities to the University. CNEs on the other hand can be based purely in the hospital setting supporting nurses wherever necessary as the need arises.

Education transcends all aspects of care delivery, Handy (1993) states that a culture of learning and support is a vital ingredient for staff morale and team building. As already stated, this applies not only to the place of work but in my case also to the wards and departments where we receive patients from or discharge to. During the winter pressures of 99/2000 the ITU services were pushed to the limit (Hind *et al.* 2000). I remember as the nurse in-charge of the unit it was particularly stressful trying to support junior members of staff and run the unit during these busy periods. I recall staff nurses on surgical and medical wards, finding it very difficult to cope with the type of patients being discharged to them from ITU because of the pressure on beds.

Often ward-based staff are very reluctant to receive patients who are being discharged from ITU when there is a bed shortage on the ward. This often leads to ever increasing difficulty in discharging patients and consequently negative media coverage. Hind *et al.* (*ibid.*) cites the London *Evening Standard* which stated that the bed crisis in ITU is 'scandalous'.

Education and training of staff is the key to addressing these issues, both within critical care and the wards. Boundaries between these areas are increasingly overlapping. Acute ward staff are being required to care for patients previously only seen in a Critical Care setting and are often ill prepared to manage such patients. High rates of staff turnover in Critical Care areas present difficulties in finding suitable preceptors for new staff, who subsequently suffer, due to inadequate support during their first year. Gibson (1996), Coad and Haines (1999) and Corr (2000) highlight lack of support as a major stress factor for all levels of staff, leading to recruitment and retention difficulties. Introducing the role of Clinical Nurse Educator to work alongside the existing lecturer practitioners, could enhance the quality of care delivery in all Critical Care settings. They could take responsibility for:

- Developing educational programmes for ward nurses and NVQ training.
- Practice development of junior ITU nurses.
- Staff development for those working flexible shifts.
- Developing additional links with universities.
- Developing core competencies in ITU nursing practice.
- Enhancing networking skills of all staff, so as to share evidence based practice both at a local and national level.
- Involvement in research and audit to improve quality of care.

Developing educational programmes for ward nurses and NVQ training

There continues to be an ever increasing demand on the existing complement of Critical Care beds and as such the need for Critical Care is now much more determined by the level of care needed rather than the location in which it is delivered (Coad & Haines *op. cit.*). As previously discussed this is a major problem for ward based nurses to address and is supported by the literature (Place & Cornock, 1997; Audit Commission, 1999; Russell, 2000). Indeed the DoH (2000) states that all ward based staff who will be caring for patients following discharge from Critical Care should have received competence based high-dependency training by March 2004.

If Clinical Nurse Educators (CNE) roles were developed they could share their knowledge and skills in Critical Care with ward based nurses. In this way much could be achieved in improving patient care on the wards. Their CNE role would involve them in advising ward based staff rather than to take over the care of the patient on the ward.

A rapidly diminishing, suitably trained workforce within Critical Care, is demanding that experienced staff demonstrate more flexible and cost effective ways of working, during times of peak and low periods of pressure. This could be achieved, through developing an appropriate dependency score, determining what level of care a patient needs and who should provide it. Experienced nurses would then be able to care for more than one patient for a shift, where appropriate, aided by a support worker or junior nurse. Hind *et al. (op. cit.)*, found that the introduction of Health Care Support Workers (HCSW) would be a viable option in this situation. Given adequate training to NVQ level they would be able to carry out certain basic nursing care procedures as well as general housekeeping and clerical duties under the supervision of qualified nurses. This would allow the qualified nurses to devote more of their time to delivering the highly skilled care to patients. This approach to delivering care may help to alleviate staffing problems, however it must be investigated thoroughly, before given serious consideration.

Practice development of junior critical care nurses

CNEs would be a great asset within Critical Care, working with junior staff to coach them in developing skills in all areas of this nursing specialty and complementing the work of the lecturer practitioners. Whilst the lecturer practitioners have at least six Critical Care areas to oversee, having a CNE working solely in one area would greatly enhance support for developing nursing skills.

When I started within ITU my mentor had been there for a number of years and was very experienced. Because there was a low staff turnover rate most of the qualified nurses there had experience and could support me in learning all aspects of Critical Care nursing. Today this is not the case. As the nurse in charge of a shift I often look around me and see that many of the nurses have less than two years experience in Critical Care and may be acting as mentors for newly qualified D grade staff nurses. These nurses are being also expected to mentor student nurses. It is therefore important that there is someone there to guide and coach both the preceptor and preceptee, in their practice development (Ashburner, 1996).

Staff development for those working flexible shifts

Further flexibility, with regard to addressing staffing problems, could be found through identifying a core of staff willing to work shifts that suit their needs and those of the unit, so avoiding over- or under-staffing. The Audit Commission (1999) and the DoH (2000) have suggested this approach to nurses' working patterns should be adopted.

However, within the unit where I work there are concerns that this approach to working patterns could mean that those who work such shifts may fall behind with their professional development. However, if CNEs were in post they would be able to work similar shifts and therefore, ensure that staff support mechanisms are being effectively utilised. Emphasis should be placed on the importance of Clinical Supervision and what it really means. Individual performance reviews should be occurring on an annual basis and personal development programmes devised as a result. All members of staff should be encouraged to embark on developing a philosophy of lifelong learning (DoH, 2002) not in reference list and to undertake leadership programs (Manthey and Miller, 1994) developed to facilitate continued development in the absence of those leading ongoing initiatives.

The DoH (1997, 1999) highlights the importance of ensuring these initiatives are implemented in the workplace and recommendations are made as to how nurses in Critical Care need to modernise working practices, enhance decision-making and leadership skills and raise quality of care within this specialty (Audit Commission, 1999; DoH, 2000).

Developing core competencies in Critical Care nursing practice

To further expand the roles of Critical Care nurses in agreed areas of practice such as, defibrillation or nurse prescribing, we must ensure that what we do already is of the best possible standard. It is important to have professional guidelines and a structured response to the increasingly blurring interfaces between medicine and nursing within Critical Care. This could be achieved through CNEs developing links with the Universities, currently providing the Critical Care specialist courses, such as the Critical Care pathway at Northumbria University. They could develop core competencies in order to train all nurses working within the specialty. This enhanced collaboration with Universities would allow a more clinical input into the education of Critical Care nurses, as well as addressing the recommendation outlined by the UKCC (1992) and Peach (1999) for those under going pre-registration education. The introduction of the lecturer-practitioner posts has already addressed these issues but could be further strengthened by introduction of CNE posts.

Charlton, Machin and Clough (2000) describe how collaboration with the Workforce Development Confederation has brought great benefits to the workplace. These benefits include the breaking down of barriers between health care providers and health education providers. They describe how they have developed core competencies in 29 clinical areas and how the development of skills training programmes beyond the traditionally accepted preceptorship period, has aided recruitment and retention of junior staff. This in-turn reduces pressure on existing staff as they do not have to worry about who is supporting the new staff, as well as deal with increasing workloads. There is a more flexible approach to learning, so allowing part-time staff to continue their professional development. Their work highlights the importance of clinical based staff working with academic establishments as the way forward to bridging the theory practice gap.

Enhancing staffs' skills in networking, audit and research at a local and national level to improve quality of care

The DoH (2000) proposes that staff in Critical Care areas should have strong networking skills. This has been addressed by 29 Regional Critical Care Network Groups being established at the beginning of 2001. In addition, Newcastle upon Tyne Hospitals NHS Trust established a Critical Care Steering Group to provide a link between all the critical care areas in the Trust. These groups are enabling common standards and protocols to be developed to prevent inequalities in the standard of care delivery at both local and national level. I believe that it will also allow for nurses to move between Critical Care areas more efficiently, knowing that working practices are standardised.

The DoH (2000) also emphasises the importance of developing a data collecting culture to help towards the promotion of evidence based practice. Collaboration with universities and all Critical Care providers will foster such a culture, and move protocols away from being based on custom and practice to being based on a sound evidence base. In order to keep abreast of all research in their area of practice a doctor would need to read 19 articles a day every day of the year (Sackett *et al.* 1996) while Parkin (1998) not in reference list points out that only 21% of medical health technology is actually evidence based.

Conclusion

The UKCC (1992) Code of Professional Conduct, clauses 3,6,14, requires nurses to, strive toward consistently high levels of practice. Whatever the title given to those nurses who aim to move practice forward in their specialist area, it is important that all nurses realise that they are a part of this change and have a role to play. Change should not be something to be afraid of, indeed Coombs (1999) reminds us that,

> *'... it is important to understand, in this rapidly changing environment, that any developments will not threaten the very essence and centrality of what we perceive nursing to be, unless we allow them to do so.'*

We need to take advantage of opportunities for change and begin to shape it into something that encompasses what is termed as the 'Essence of Nursing' (Kitson, 1999).

As I learnt to reflect upon the ongoing educational needs of nurses in Critical Care I realised that I had begun the process of 'learning about my own learning' and as a result I am now better able to influence the way in which my colleagues will learn in the future. While I worked towards achieving my various learning outcomes for the AWBL I became aware that as a profession we are not very good at recognising what we contribute to our clinical areas. The AWBL journey has made me more questioning of my practice and that of others in my team.

I now realise that nurses play a role in patient care that is of equal importance to that of other professional groups. In the past Critical Care was based upon the 'Medical Model', but there is now more emphasis on the importance of multi-professional team working and so I believe that it is important for nurses to recognise for themselves the importance of their contribution to this team. The reflective skills I acquired and developed during the AWBL process have enabled me to look more critically at these issues. As a result I believe that nurses ought to become proactive instead of reactive in developing practice and so take more control of the destiny of the nursing profession.

References

Ashburner, C. (1996) 'Pitfalls of preceptorship and the need for adequate supervision.' *Nursing in Critical Care* (1, 6) pp. 296–301.

Audit Commission (1999) *Critical to success* (Audit Commission, London).

Bowman, M. (1986) *Nursing Management and Education: a Conceptual Approach to Change* (Croom Helm, London).

Burns, C. (1982) *Self-concept development and education* (Holt, Rinehart & Winston, London).

Charlton, R., Machin, S. and Clough, A. (2000) 'Collaborating with the consortium: the development of a foundation in critical care skills programme.' *Nursing in Critical Care* 5 (2) pp. 62–67.

Closs, S. and Cheater, F. (1999) 'Evidence for nursing practice: a clarification of the issues.' *Journal of Advanced Nursing* 30 (1) pp. 10–17.

Coad, S. and Haines, D. (1999) 'Supporting staff caring for critically ill patients in acute care areas.' *Nursing in Critical Care* (4, 5) pp. 245–48.

Coombs, M. (1999) 'The challenge facing critical care nurses in the UK: a personal perspective.' *Nursing in Critical Care* 4(2) pp. 81–4.

Corr, M. (2000) 'Reducing occupational stress in intensive care.' *Nursing in Critical Care* 5 (2) pp. 76–80.

Department of Health (1997) *The New NHS: Modern and Dependable* (The Stationery Office, London).

Department of Health (1999) *Making a Difference* (The Stationery Office, London).

Department of Health (2000) *Comprehensive Critical Care* (The Stationery Office, London).

Gibson, J. (1996) 'Afraid of Critical Care?' *Nursing Standard* 11 (11) p. 20.

Gibson, J. (1997) 'Focus of Nursing in critical and acute care settings: prevention or cure?' *Intensive and Critical Care Nursing* 13(3) pp. 163–166.

Handy, C. (1993) *Understanding organisations* (Penguin Books, London).

Haynes, S. (1992) 'Let the change come from within: the process of change in nursing.' *Professional Nurse* 7(10) pp. 635–638.

Hinchliff, S. (1999) *The Practitioner Teacher* (Bailliere Tindall, London).

Hind, M., Jackson, D., Andrews, C., Fulbrook, P., Galvin, K. and Frost, S. (2000) 'Health Care Support Workers in the Critical Care Setting.' *Nursing in Critical Care* 5 (1) pp. 31–39.

Johns, C. (1995) 'Framing learning through reflection within Carper's fundamental ways of knowing in nursing.' *Journal of Advanced Nursing* 22 pp. 226–34.

Kember, D., Kam Yuet Wong, F. and Young, E. (2001) 'The nature of reflection in Kember *et al.*' (eds) *Reflective Teaching and Learning in the Health Professions* (Blackwell, Oxford).

Kitson, A. (1999) 'The Essence of Nursing.' *Nursing Standard* 13 (24) pp. 43–6.

Lancaster, J. and Lancaster, W. (1982) *The nurse as a change agent* (CV. Mosby, St Louis).

Manthey, M. and Miller, D. (1994) *Leading an Empowered Organisation* (Creative Healthcare Management, Minneapolis).

Mauksch, I. and Miller, M. (1981) *Implementing change in nursing* (CV. Mosby, St Louis).

Morison, M. (1992) 'Promoting the motivation to change, the role of facilitative leadership in quality assurance.' *Professional Nurse* 7 (11) pp. 715–718.

Peach, L. (1999) *Fitness for Practice* (UKCC, London).

Place, B. and Cornock, M. (1997) 'Care is critical: critical timing.' *Nursing Times* 93 (26) pp. 26–27.

Russell, S. (2000) 'Continuity of care after discharge from ICU.' *Professional Nurse* 15 (8) pp. 497–500.

Sackett, D., Rosenberg, W., Muir-Gray, J., Haynes, B. and Richardson, S. (1996) 'Evidence-based medicine: what it is and what it isn't.' *British Medical Journal* 312 (7023) pp. 71–2.

Schon, D. (1987) *Developing the Reflective Practitioner* (Jossey-Bass, New York).

Smith, Galenist, L. and Manthey, M. (1995) 'Improving patient outcomes through system change.' *Journal of Nursing Administration* 25 (5) pp. 55–63.

Tross, G. and Cavanagh, S. (1996) 'Innovation in nursing management: professional, management and methodological considerations.' *Journal of Nursing Management* 24 (4) pp. 143–149.

United Kingdom Central Council for Nursing, Midwifery and Health Visiting (1999) *Fitness for Practice* (The UKCC Commission for Nursing and Midwifery Education, London).

Wong, S. (1978) 'Nurse-teachers' behaviours in the clinical field: apparent effect on nursing students learning.' *Journal of Advanced Nursing* 3 (3) pp. 369–372.

Wragg, E.C. (1994) *Classroom teaching skills* (Croom Helm, London).

Chapter 9

Valuing learning in a Masters programme of study

John Miller, Margaret Best and Jill Robson

Introduction

This chapter discusses the work based learning that arose within a tripartite learning contract, which was part of a practice project completed by Jill Robson while undertaking an MA Advanced Practice programme. The project, undertaken within a National Health Service Trust, was developed to meet the assessment criteria for the programme and was negotiated within a tripartite learning contract by John, Margaret and Jill. The project addressed specified characteristics of advanced practice, which were explicit within the MA programme. These included risk, empowerment, change management and leadership. A central theme running through the project is 'Patient Focused Care (PFC)' which besides being relevant to the programme of study is a new concept of patient care and management being introduced into the Trust. The experience of developing and completing this project will be discussed from the perspectives of the student (Jill) who is a senior nurse in the Trust, the Director of Nursing in the Trust (Margaret) and the Educational Supervisor from Northumbria University (John).

The development of a new academic award at Northumbria University, the MA Advanced Practice attempted to break with acknowledged practice and create a 'Practice Project' for students to undertake as their substantive piece of assessed work. A characteristic of Masters study is the requirement for postgraduate students to demonstrate achievement of 'masters outcomes' in an earned piece of work. Whether it is called a dissertation or a thesis the traditional approach is to undertake an empirical study. Supported by a research supervisor, the student adhering to the stages of the research process develops their study, using one or other of the research paradigms. The difference the Practice Project has brought to Masters study is its emphasis on changing practice by a practitioner in collaboration with others, while also meeting competence in advanced practice. However, both the Practice Project and empirical study place similar expectations upon the student. Both have a supervisor, both expect the student to liaise and link with someone in practice while the completed assignment for both pieces of work, will be around 12,000 to 15,000 words.

The process the student follows in the practice projects mirrors what Lewin (1946) suggested is a circular process for action research, of planning, executing and fact finding for evaluation. It has been argued by many authors (Hart & Bond, 1995; Webb, 1991; Holloway & Wheeler, 1996) that one of the most useful and frequent types of research in nursing is Action Research. They suggest that researchers who use this method believe in creating change in the setting they investigate and in nursing this means the identification of a specific problem in clinical or educational practice and trying to change this with the aim of improving the situation. Webb (1991) states that action research is a way of doing research and working on problems at the same time.

The historical background of action research has its origins in the educational problem-solving approach of the 1940s in the USA. Lewin (1951) suggested a circular process for action research, which includes planning, executing and fact finding for evaluation. Holloway and Wheeler (1996) citing Meyer (1993), suggest that modern nurse researchers have translated Lewin's ideas into a framework with several stages: planning, acting, observing and reflecting. Holter and Schwartz-Barkott (1993) give four characteristics of action research: collaboration, between researcher and practitioner, solution of practical problems, change in practice and the development of theory. They argue that the four elements are necessary for successful action research and that without collaboration, changes in practice cannot be made and therefore problems will remain unsolved.

The practice project has been until recently spread over three modules of learning. Within the MA Advanced Practice their completion is seen as central to demonstrating competence in advanced practice. Competence in this instance refers to the integration of knowledge, perceptions, values and professional practice skills necessary for advanced and advancing practice. A key arrangement for undertaking the Practice Project is a 'tripartite contract', established between the student, a peer from their practice area and an academic supervisor. The student is seen as the driver behind the contract and is responsible for organising meetings between all parties.

In this instance, Jill as the student was responsible for developing the project and driving it forward. The overall aim of the project was to raise the quality of patient care through the implementation of a more efficient and effective multidisciplinary approach. Jill, a ward sister, had accepted the challenge to use her ward as a pilot site to implement and evaluate the concepts of multi-skilling and multidisciplinary single documentation. Therefore, as well as having to create an action plan it was her responsibility to set up meetings with all members of the tripartite learning contract. Margaret, Jill's peer from her practice area, in many respects a professional facilitator, was also the Trust's Director of Nursing and Quality. It was important that Jill not only viewed Margaret as a sounding board to explore ideas but also as someone who could help move the project along. In many respects this professional facilitator role should be seen as one which will be able to open avenues and help legitimise aspects of the project as it unfolds. John's role as the educationalist was primarily to encourage Jill to meet the criteria of her action plan, and link what was happening in the project to outcomes identified within the characteristics of advanced practice.

The idea of educationalists and practitioners working together within the parameters of a learning contract is for some an unfamiliar concept. In reality, an essential element of work-based learning is the transactional dynamic between practitioner, a practice facilitator and an educationalist. Referred to, as the 'tripartite learning contract' the emphasis placed on this relationship is one of partnership and collaboration. It is, however, important to acknowledge different dimensions to the word collaboration. Collaborative learning within the context of the learning contract is seen as an opportunity for practitioners to work alongside an educationalist to grasp subject matter and deepen their understanding of it. During this process, which is seen as essentially practical in nature, practitioners are inevitably developing their social and intellectual skills (Bruffee, 1987; McKinley, 1983; MacGregor 1990).

It could be argued that much of the literature suggests collaborative learning occurs in classroom settings between students and teacher, although it would appear that the principles identified above are equally appropriate when applied to groups of learners in other more practical environments.

Gokhale (1999) argues that proponents of collaborative learning claim the active exchange of ideas within such a collaborative group not only increases interest among the participants but also promotes critical thinking. Totten *et al.* (1991) suggest that such shared learning gives practitioners (as in this case) an opportunity to engage in discussion, take responsibility for their own learning and thus become critical thinkers. MacGregor (1990) suggests that social constructionism, an expanding web of epistemological perspectives in several disciplines, arises from the assumption that knowledge is socially rather than individually, constructed by communities of individuals. Knowledge is shaped over time by successive conversations and by ever changing social and political environments.

McKinley (1980) makes the assumption that collaborative learning is a discussion in which learners co-operate in identifying and exploring the nature and perceived adequacy of each others perceptions, opinions and beliefs in a given area of study. The discussion, he argues, is to help each member of the group identify and examine the nature and basis of their understanding and the possibilities of alternative views.

The role of the educationalist in collaborative learning especially in the context of the tripartite learning contract does take on a different set of values from the traditional pedagogical teaching role. From a didactic to facilitative – learning role, ensures that besides having a set of 'teacher' responsibilities, the educationalist also has to be open, sharing and flexible enough to accept others perceptions, opinions and beliefs.

Collaborating with health care professionals is certainly not a new concept. The strength of the health care curriculum over many years has relied heavily on academics and practitioners working together to create valid and reliable programmes of study. Dearing (1997) stated that Higher Education (HE) must increase its contribution to the economy and its responsiveness to the needs of business. If the needs of business are for cost-effective flexible training the only way HE can be seen to be delivering is through collaborative working arrangements that have to be present in new ways of working.

The three practice projects, undertaken by Jill within the context of the MA Advanced Practice, were completed over a two-year period and equated to 60 academic credits at Masters level. It is the largest piece of work the student completes and in addition to 'contract' meetings arranged by the student in their practice area, there is also additional support sessions incorporated into the timetable during semesters. Initially the student is required to provide and negotiate (within the context of the tripartite contract) an overarching plan for their project focusing on an issue or problem within their practice setting. This includes a critical analysis and assessment of the working context and an evidence based rationale. It is also important to include resources necessary for the project and evidence of concept and theory analysis as the basis for purposeful decision-making.

As the Practice Project unfolds, the student identifies and demonstrates a growing breadth and depth of the essential knowledge base, values and workplace/practice skills to meet their objectives and the characteristics of advanced practice. Further integration of theories and their critical analysis and synthesis will facilitate such growth. Reflection on and in practice, supported by discussion and debate in both the work/practice place and University enables the student to examine and challenge taken for granted practice assumptions. The anticipated personal and professional development the student experiences enable them to expand upon their project initiatives. This includes the harnessing and development of colleague's skills and the optimum use of other resources necessary for the progress of the project. In the final stages of the Practice Project they are encouraged to reflect and act upon the projects' development and its effect upon the organisation, e.g. policy formation and the practitioner's contribution. At this stage, it is seen as important that the student is able to contribute to the policy, business plan or strategy for the organisation. An aspect of the project must be evaluated or an evaluation/audit tool designed and piloted. While it is expected that the student is able to demonstrate discernment, in relation to how the project can be sustained given the contextual influences. At this stage it is expected that all characteristics of advanced practice will have been achieved.

The characteristics of advanced practice are integral to the tripartite learning agreement, established between the student, a peer from their organisation and the academic supervisor. The characteristics Jill had to achieve focused on:

- Assessment and risk taking.
- Advancement of nursing skills and the utilisation of skills of transfer.
- Leadership, assertiveness and decision-making.
- Empowerment of colleagues, facilitation of professional development, teaching and supervision.
- Organisational change and development.
- Implementation and evaluation of quality outcomes.

All three practice projects Jill undertook did provide an innovative opportunity for her to utilise her achievement of competence, and to build on such competence by developing a sustainable initiative in the area of Practice Development within her own practice setting.

The practice projects had been developed from a belief that critical reflective skills, inherent in all postgraduate modules and courses are the foundation on which you can progress an initiative within the context of a practice project and demonstrate in a tangible way how it can be sustained for the benefit of colleagues and the furtherance of the professions knowledge base. In today's health and social care settings, practitioners are not only engaged in the practice of their profession, but also in supporting the environment as an active learning arena, where students and professionals are expected to develop and maintain their competence in very complex situations. The focus of the practice projects is therefore to implement and evaluate a practice initiative or change, which has an impact on improving practice/practitioner development, while exploring the individuals own role as a practitioner in effecting change.

Jill's account of the development work she undertook in her practice does reflect how practice initiatives are acted upon and also how such initiatives can be used successfully within the context of an academic piece of work, or as in this case the three practice projects forming part of an MA Advanced Practice Award.

Jill recounted:

'I was first introduced to the term 'Patient Focused Care (PFC)' in June 1994. During a telephone conversation with my immediate senior manager I was asked if I would consider a seven-day trip to the United States to visit approximately 12 hospitals, which were already delivering this new system of care. I was informed that the plans for our new hospital were being changed from a nucleus design and a PFC design was now being explored. This visit evolved into a very positive experience for me that inspired me to reflect upon our whole system of care delivery. On my return to England I began to question everything we did, the way we did it and why we did things that way.

Reflecting on my practice (Schon, 1983; Boud *et al.* 1985; Powell, 1989; Smith & Russell, 1991; Johns, 1993, 1995) lead to a critical analysis of the service we provided and feelings of disillusion with the complexity of systems in place. This critical analysis of practice provided the stimulus to move on and try new perspectives. The NHS reforms (DoH, 1977, 1998), a change in government and rationalisation of our hospital caused some concern within the Trust and for a time the original plans for the implementation of PFC were shelved. However, as a unit we already had commenced the pilot and been impressed with the concept so decided to carry on.

As the ward manager I took the role of project leader and acted as the agent of change. Having already commenced the MA Advanced Practice degree, I decided that the aim of the three practice projects over a two-year period was to complete the implementation of the concepts of PFC, evaluate the outcomes and if successful assist other wards and departments with the implementation of change.

The overall aim of this project was to raise the quality of patient care through the implementation of a more efficient and effective multidisciplinary approach. Acting as the agent of change it was my responsibility to create the environment, education and support necessary to facilitate the team in their personal development to create the change in practice. I had to assess and minimise the risk to patients and staff from change itself and evaluate the outcomes from a patient, professional and organisational view.

The change involved the implementation and evaluation of the concepts of PFC. Having analysed the literature surrounding PFC (Booze-Allen & Hamilton, 1988; Garside, 1993; Heyman & Culling, 1994; Hurst, 1995) our team volunteered to be a pilot site to implement and evaluate the concepts of multi-skilling and multidisciplinary single documentation. Multi-skilling was chosen from our constant frustration with delays awaiting medical staff or technicians to perform daily skills such as venepuncture and electrocardiograph tracing. This training it was hoped would create a broader skill base for nurses, while increasing patient contact time and reducing the amount of contacts for each patient. Multidisciplinary single document and pathways of care were chosen to try and reduce documentation time by preventing duplication of records and also to develop a more multidisciplinary approach to providing clinically effective care. If the evaluation was positive the intention was for myself to assist with the roll out to other wards and departments within the Trust. The three practice projects were therefore the vehicle we would use to complete the pilot and evaluate the changes made in practice.

Practice Project One involved evaluation of the present position, completion and implementation of a pathway of care for each diagnosis within the speciality (which happened to be plastic surgery) and the creation of a multidisciplinary single document, acceptable to all professions.

Practice Project Two involved the negotiation and implementation of in-service training requirements to continue multi-skilling for qualified and unqualified staff. Having previously implemented skills including venepuncture, cannulation and electrocardiograph tracing, it was also considered important to include nurse prescribing. The development of the unqualified staff (team assistants) also continued through a pilot project of National Vocational Qualification Level 3 in care to continue the multi-skilling of the unqualified staff. As part of my own

professional development and advancing my practice I decided as part
of the multi-skilling concept to commence patient assessment and
evaluation for pre-operative assessment and look at the feasibility of
nurse prescribing within protocols.

Practice Project Three involved a reflective account of the introduction
of PFC and evaluation of changes made in practice.

By the time Practice Project One was completed, through sheer
perseverance and the use of my own communication, leadership and
reflective skills; as well as the hard work and support of the rest of my
team, we had developed 18 pathways of care, a multidisciplinary single
document and following the presentation of the single document to
medical records and the request to try and reduce documentation
further we also finished up piloting a re-admission document. Having
started this project with a greater level of resistance to change than
drivers for change (Lewin, 1951) I felt a great sense of achievement after
Practice Project One and began to assist other wards in the Trust with
the implementation of multidisciplinary documentation and multi-
skilling.

The second major part in implementing PFC was undertaking Practice
Project Two. This involved incorporating leadership, assertiveness,
empowerment and supervisory skills in the planning, training and
implementation of a programme of multi-skilling to facilitate the
individual to meet the organisational goals. These expanded and
extended roles and moved professional boundaries to provide more
efficient and effective care and improved service delivery. This erosion
of professional boundaries however brought with it the confusion of
accountability and the anxieties involved in changing roles. By the
completion of Practice Project Two we had successfully implemented a
range of extended roles for registered nurses and team assistants. These
skills included venepuncture, cannulation advanced cardiac life support,
electrocardiograph tracing and male catheterisation. The development
of the unqualified staff (team assistants) was processed through a pilot
project for the Trust using the National Vocational Qualification Level 3
training in care. As part of my own professional development and
advancing my practice I commenced pre-operative patient assessment
incorporating knowledge from the clinical assessment unit, delivered as
part of the MA Advanced Practice programme of study. My decision for
including this extended role was to continue the nurse practitioner role
for pre-operative assessment during holidays and absence.

Although the PFC project was an organisational goal, the decision to pilot the concept within our unit was mine. I began with an autocratic leadership style and told the staff we would be piloting the project, and then through a process of education and sharing my vision, the project became a team objective. At first my aim was to try and extend the registered nurse and team assistant role through a process of in-service training in certain skills or task acquisition. Each team member was given the opportunity to expand their role through a process of education, supervision and support empowering and enabling them to change practice.

My aim did become extended to encourage and support each individual within the team to continuously develop their clinical knowledge, assessment and decision-making skills to enable them not only to carry out these skills but to assess the patient and decide when they are required. Nursing development should not be limited to extending the role but more importantly it must address autonomy and accountability in practice.

As the ward manager I took the role of project leader and acted as the agent of change (Allen, 1993; Cahill, 1995; Lancaster 1999), challenging the status quo using reflection (Johns, 1995; Smith & Russell, 1991) on present practice. While the literature suggests there are varying approaches to change, I believe at some point throughout the project I have had to adopt them all to assist the implementation of the project.

The first part of Practice Project Three involved a reflective account considering the implementation of PFC within the unit, while I critically analysed different theories of change in an attempt to understand the process of change and the reactions of the individuals involved.

The second part of this Practice Project evaluated changes made in practice while I tried to understand the difference if any, these changes made to the stakeholders involved. The main stakeholders being the patient as the receiver of care, the staff as the deliverer of that care and the organisation responsible for providing that care. A number of previous evaluations (Garside, 1993; Heyman & Culling, 1994; Hurst, 1995) to date have consisted of outcome measures, concerned with how far the intervention meets stated objectives or goals, mainly from an organisational perspective. The evaluation undertaken within Practice Project Three used a pluralistic approach (Ovretveit, 1998) to achieve explanation and understanding from all three stakeholders perspectives.

The team were motivated and enthused by the concept and began to act as a driving force (Lewins, 1951) for change disturbing the equilibrium or status quo of present practice. With the support of the Trust board for training and their agreement to create multidisciplinary pathways of care I believed the environment for change was ripe. The Director of Nursing created a Patient Focused Care steering group with representation from training and development, human resources, medicine and nursing. We were given the freedom to choose the aspects of PFC we wanted to pilot and adapt it to our area as we saw fit. The steering group acted as our organisational authority and enabled the project, reducing organisational constraints, for example, allowing us to create our own documentation and piloting it without medical records approval.

At a unit level I created a large multidisciplinary group of nurses (registered and team assistants), doctors, physiotherapists, occupational therapists, and anaesthetists, including representatives (nurses) from the outpatient wound care clinic and theatres. The objectives for this group were to agree the extended/expanded roles of the multidisciplinary team and the required training. Secondly, to discuss variances in practice, and incorporate evidence based care (DoH, 1997) into the creation of a multidisciplinary pathway of care for each diagnosis cared for within the unit. I was aiming for collaboration between all professionals and a joint decision-making process to create collective responsibility for our outcomes (Liedtka & Whitten, 1996).

The first meeting of this group, however, did not go according to plan. Although all parties had agreed with the idea, instead of collaboration, intra-group conflict arose (Sullivan & Decker, 1997). The medical staff were quite happy with the multi-skilling aspect and fairly keen to give away tasks such as venepuncture, cannulation, ECG, and male catheterisation. They were, however, quite aggressive towards multidisciplinary pathways of care and the challenge it presented to their practice, and I suspect their authority, supporting the view that medical staff will give away what they want to, but still want to hold overall control (Leifers, 1995). The physiotherapists and occupational therapists were concerned regarding role erosion and indignant that they must keep separate records to assist out-patient follow up appointments.

This was the first and strongest resistance to the change I experienced, caused I believe by a lack of understanding of multi-skilling and multidisciplinary pathways of care, a reluctance to acknowledge their practice was less than perfect, and their belief that change implies criticism (Allen, 1993). The meeting developed into a battle of power. The medical staff tried to exercise what they believed to be their legitimate power (French & Raven, 1959; Lancaster, 1999) to prevent the project any further. I tried to reduce their resistance using my knowledge of PFC and the advantages it had to offer them, such as reducing length of stay (Wilson, 1997) and creating the framework for implementing evidence based practice (DoH, 1997) to sell the idea. Negotiating with professionals who have been historically senior to nursing can however prove to be quite difficult (May, 1997). I continued to use negotiation, questioning their objections and inviting alternatives to explore and improve practice. On reflection at times I know I was struggling to maintain communicating in the adult ego, (Berne, 1966) trying to prevent their attempts to control the meeting. I managed to control my responses, through recognition of their pre-contemplation stage of change (Prochaska *et al.* 1992), unaware of the present problems with variances in practice, and their belief that there was no need to change. They would require education of the principles of PFC and careful reflection of their practice to accept that there was room for improvement. I was not confident, however, at that stage that I was the individual to do this.

The confrontation and resistance to change that I had avoided with my own staff through education of the idea and their involvement, I unfortunately hit head on with the medical staff, physiotherapists and occupational therapists. They were not allowing me the opportunity to sell them the idea and I felt overpowered by their resistance. I continued to try and communicate the concept to assist their visualisation and reduce their anxieties. Although I was disappointed with my ability to motivate the group and create some enthusiasm, I was quite pleased with my determination, which lead to their eventual agreement that we (the nurses) could pilot multi-skilling and multidisciplinary pathways of care. On reflection I am not sure if this compromise was agreed out of trust and respect for my perseverance as referent power (Lancaster, 1999) or sympathy for the subordinate. They had not rejected (Rogers & Schoemaker, 1971) the change project entirely, and I accepted that they would be the late adapters or laggards in responding to the change. I did have the support of my own team and the power of the collective subordinates, in this case the nursing staff, should not be underestimated (Lancaster, 1999). While legitimate and expert power are useful attributes for change, agent resilience and perseverance are essential.

I created two groups of staff to look at multidisciplinary pathways of care and multi-skilling from volunteers or innovators (Rogers & Schoemaker, 1971), who were curious, eager and enthusiastic towards the project and we began the implementation (Sullivan & Decker, 1988) or moving phase (Lewins, 1951) from the bottom up.

The extended roles for the qualified and unqualified nurses were considered carefully exploring areas that would improve the patients care. The education and training needs required were also carefully considered to ensure confidence and competence to practice (UKCC, 1992). Although there are several accounts of implementing Patient Focused Care within the literature (Deggerhammer & Wade, 1991; Layton, 1993; Morgan, 1993; Routh & Stafford, 1996) and the advantages and disadvantages of the model (Eubanks, 1991; Minnen *et al.* 1993; Porter O'Grady, 1993; Townsend, 1993), training issues are mentioned only briefly. The majority of individual nurses were very positive and eager to begin extending their roles supporting Maggenis *et al.* (1999) findings, others were more concerned regarding taking on the doctors' work, their increased exposure to litigation and their confidence and competence in carrying out the skills. There was also concern regarding the loss of their 'essential caring role', which supported Kitson's (1999) findings. As we began the training, I realised that the development of the individuals within the team and the necessary change in attitude towards their accountability and responsibility in managing patient care was more important than the skill acquisition itself (Routh & Stafford, 1996; Ford 1997, Jenner, 1998). I remained flexible allowing individuals to move along their own continuum of 'follower readiness' (Hersheys life cycle cited in Grohar-Murray & Dicroce, 1997, p. 30). The more enthusiastic and motivated individuals and myself were trained first, allowing the "unable, unwilling or insecure" practitioners to follow when they had progressed to the "willing, able and confident" stage. As more staff were trained, the motivation of others increased and the confident and competent practitioners supported the newly trained members of the team, building teamwork, trust and empowerment of others (Kouze & Posner, 1997).

The literature acknowledges the confusion arising from extended and expanded roles and the erosion of professional boundaries (Dowling *et al.* 1995; Devine, 1995; Leonard, 1999; Jones & Davies, 1999) and the legal, ethical and professional complexities that arose (Parker & Wilson, 1992; Dimond, 1995; Tingle, 1998; Jones & Davies, 1999). I was aiming for professional collaboration (Moyse, 1993) and rather than concentrating on eroding boundaries I was trying to develop staff raising the educational level of all the professionals to increase their flexibility and subsequently improve the quality of patient care (O'Brian & Stepura, 1992; Brider, 1992; Southwick, 1993). As the ward manager I also had to be sure that each individual was confident and competent to practice, aware of his or her legal, ethical and professional responsibility and accountability in protecting the public.

The second group, developing multidisciplinary pathways of care began with a goal to create two pathways of care for our most common surgical diagnosis. To improve communication of the project and involve the late adopters, laggards and rejecters (Rogers & Schoemaker, 1971) we evaluated the first 20 pathways, asking ourselves what was going right? What could be better? (Doerge & Hagenow, 1995, p. 32). We decided to change course and created a multidisciplinary admission document (Appendix 30) and a pathway of care for each diagnosis (Appendix 31).

Attempting to reduce the medical staffs' resistance and decrease their combined legitimate power I discussed the pathways with them individually and challenged their care against the literature and each other to achieve agreement on best practice. Other less formidable restraining forces (Lewin, 1951) to the project included, time to set up the pathways and the new documentation. The goal was to have a pathway of care for each diagnosis which would allow us to throw away altogether the nursing process documentation, letting go of the old and integrating the new as accepted practice. According to Lewin (1951) this is known as 'refreezing'.

The final part of any change is of course the evaluation to prove the success or failure of the project. To date we have achieved our original aims to create 19 pathways of care and a multidisciplinary admission document and the nursing process has been entirely abolished. We have also accomplished a programme of multi-skilling for registered and team assistant nurses. The purpose of any evaluation is to assess the effects and effectiveness of an innovation or intervention in policy practice or service (Robson, 1997).

The project has involved many major changes for the unit and the evaluation of these changes has been quite difficult. Recognising the three main stakeholders required measurement of success from three perspectives, the organisation, the staff and the patients. The evaluation combined both process and outcome measurements. Admittedly the literature surrounding research and evaluation of health care is extremely vast and the arguments for and against quantitative and qualitative methods have caused me, as one practice evaluator, some concern. Being sceptical of the validity of action research at first I have now come to terms with this methodology as an answer to the evaluation of nursing practice. I believe it does promote the development of the nurse as the "practitioner researcher" (Hart, 1995) by empowering nurses to bring about changes in practice while evaluating at the same time (Titchen & Binnie, 1993; Newton, 1995). I believe as suggested that action research may well be the answer to the theory practice gap (Holtzer & Scwar-Barcott, 1993; Titchen, 1995). Although it is becoming more widely used in health care (East & Robinson, 1994) according to Hart (1995) it has been a recognised research methodology for over 50 years since first described by Lewin (1946). Perhaps the slow response has been attributable to the difficulties that have been associated with validity in qualitative research (Parahoo, 1997). As Titchen (1995) points out there are a number of tests one can apply to test truth and reality using self and participant evaluation, the final test of validity, however, being the degree to which the research is useful in guiding practice and its power to inform and precipitate debate, for improving practice (Lomax, 1986).

A participatory approach using interviews allowed us to interpret and understand the meaning of the changes made to ourselves (the staff) and the patients. The participation of the staff thus minimising the gap between what is researched and what is practised, allowing immediate changes to be made where appropriate to improve care (Wallis, 1998).

Using a developmental approach of action research (Hart 1995; Ovretveit, 1998; Allan & Cornes, 1998), reflection in action allowed us to reshape what we were doing, while we were doing it (Jarvis, 1992). Difficulties in maintaining the competence of all staff in venepuncture arose; we therefore had to reduce the amount of people with the skill to increase their practice. We decided to stop the team assistants training in venepuncture while at the same time added other skills not originally included such as blood glucose monitoring and naso-gastric tube feeding. The multidisciplinary pathways of care also had several changes along the way as problems with staff compliance, or the patients under-standing of the nursing language was highlighted by the users.

As the change project has reached completion and having attempted some evaluation, with hindsight, much more thought should have been given to the evaluation design, what would be measured and the agreed criteria to be used as yardsticks before we ever began the changes (Philips *et al.* 1994). As with any action research implemented in the real world however, you are not always entirely sure what the changes will mean, although we had hoped to achieve some of the advantages already listed in the literature (Hurst, 1995; Redman & Jones, 1998). The changes are now well established as part of our everyday practice and this is perhaps the true value of action research. There is no regression to our original state and no difficulties with implementing our findings into practice as implementation has evolved along the way.

Alternative data collection methods for patient and staff satisfaction could have been the standard questionnaire survey. Although a larger sample could have been used than in interview data collection, the closed question technique is criticised for obtaining less critical responses compared to open ended questions indicating an inappropriately high satisfaction with care (Bowling, 1992). There are also a number of ready-made satisfaction tools available such as the Newcastle Satisfaction with Nursing Care Scale (Walsh & Walsh, 1999), and as indicated earlier the Trust already has its own. The problem with ready-made tools are that they do not always aim specifically at the data required (Roth, 1998), but could be used as a starting point.'

Jill's account does highlight the many issues surrounding practice development in contemporary health care today. Not only are there issues within the nursing profession, but across professional boundaries when introducing something as complex as Patient Focused Care. The account reflects the process as it happened to Jill. However because she was also using the experience as part of the three practice projects within the MA Advanced Practice she had established her tripartite learning contract. A key stakeholder within this practice initiative was the Director of Nursing, Margaret, but besides having an organisational interest in the introduction of PFC, Margaret was also the peer from Jill's practice environment and part of the tripartite learning contract Jill had established. It's quite interesting to see how Margaret viewed this role.

Margaret:

'When Jill asked me to be her mentor for a Masters degree I accepted immediately, although in truth I had a number of conflicting emotions. I had supported a number of students taking basic degrees and knew how disillusioned they could become trying to work and having to study what often seemed to be unrelated subjects. Things improved when I was told there would be recognition of learning from the work place, although I had doubts as to how this would translate into reality.

Then there was the dreaded tripartite learning contract. So many staff had adverse experiences of this in relation either for themselves as a student, or in relation to undergraduate students on clinical placements.

For me as Director of Nursing this was a vital time in the Trust. We were building a new hospital, which was designed around our agreed model of care, i.e. Patient Focused Care. I and a cross section of staff, particularly clinical ward based staff, had explored the theories of PFC and had then developed modifications to this which became the accepted North Durham Model of Care for the new Hospital.

To introduce this new approach required moving the whole organisation to a new way of working, new systems of documentation, a total changed approach to thinking about how care was carried out. Jill had been part of the original Task Group, which developed the model, and was one of those who visited America to see Patient Focused Care in action. She was piloting the process in her existing ward. I wondered just how much more this dynamic and enthusiastic ward Sister could take on and could I keep pace with her!? However, I knew it was an opportunity to see the practice changes assessed against the theories of change management, negotiation, and acceptability. Besides realising that it would give credibility amongst those who wished to assess practice academically, I also wanted to seize the opportunity for Jill's hard work to be acknowledged, and saw it as another strand in my aim of raising the profile of ward sisters amongst other clinicians and within the region. Jill, I knew, had the ability to achieve a Master's degree.

My objectives were therefore:

- To make the tripartite learning contract viable and meaningful.
- To support Jill through the ups and downs of academia and to assist by removing any obstacles quickly when she met, inevitably in my opinion, medical or organisational opposition or blockages.
- To transfer Jill's learning into our Trust working groups and *vice versa*. This would assist the success of the small group of pilot wards and would enable the Trust to develop appropriated leaning modules, which could be rolled out across the Trust in preparation for opening of the new Hospital.
- To empower Sisters to embrace Advanced Practice, and acknowledge how they, and particularly Jill were, or could, lead the field in the Nursing Profession.

The tripartite relationship very soon became an important focus for managing the way in which we considered the workplace learning. As a group we had the advantage that all of us had met in other work/ education situations but we built on this to meet as equals. John, Jill and I met at regular intervals, making Shotley Bridge Hospital our base. We tried to see that we always arranged the next date to meet before we left, but we also limited the time spent to a maximum of two hours.

Forming a group is never easy unless the members can meet frequently for a period of time. However, because of the sense of purpose which we all brought to our group, and our reliance on each other for each person's specific skills, this process worked as a support and forward looking alliance. Jill and John challenged me regularly on risk, ethical and legal issues and I had to make what I hope were considered and wise decisions for the future of patient care within the Trust. We needed to be certain that, whilst expanding roles and pushing back barriers at what sometimes felt a vast rate, each nurse would work within the parameters of their code of professional conduct, and feel competent for each stage of development. Jill needed to recognise the different speed at which individuals worked or embraced change, and adjust accordingly. I needed to be accountable as the Professional Head of Nursing, as a Director of the Trust, and as a nurse, for all the advice that I gave. This was particularly important when allowing Jill to develop the roles of nurses in tasks previously undertaken by doctors, although this was always proposed for the benefit of patients. There were also industrial relations issues to be considered as we blurred the roles between vocational trained staff and registered staff, at what had been the previously firm lines of demarcation .The new model of care also absorbed management of the domestic, catering and portering role into the ward team and therefore under the management of Jill as Ward Sister. With the advent of more recent government initiatives, this seems insignificant now, but was radical when we developed this thinking and began to pilot this in practice.

There were occasions when Jill tackled hurdles, which caused us great debate as she moved through the stages to final resolution. The issue of a single patient record caused the medical staff great anxiety. Jill shared with us the many frequently rehearsed arguments presented to her by Senior Consultants who were anxious that they would lose the simplicity of sequential notes written by doctors. Our aim was to remove repetition for the patient. Her personal and professional standing with these members of the clinical team contributed to her success, as did her tenacity, but there is no doubt in my mind that having sound base theory and research, gained in her course, to draw upon, and the support of the tripartite group to listen, helped her to reach the ultimate goal.

I took immense pride in watching Jill deal with problems in multidiscipline Trust-wide debates. Her presentations to staff and visitors were superb, especially as by this time she was able to ask her Consultant colleagues to publicly voice commitment to the improved documentation. Junior Doctors loved the simplicity and the time saved by not repeating previous assessments.

In the long run physiotherapists were a harder group to bring on board. Indeed, even one year after implementation I know that there will be duplicate patient records somewhere in the Physiotherapy Department! In addition, particular individuals were very loath to be involved in training, to allow registered and vocationally trained staff to acquire skills for the many rehabilitation tasks they must undertake in the evenings and at weekends. Jill demonstrated to us how she worked to blur the roles on both sides. Ultimately, in her team the physiotherapists' acquired skills in dressings following plastic surgery to allow them to proceed with therapy without waiting for a nurse and other team members were given an understanding of the dynamics of mobilisation.

Thus we as a group, listened to and helped, Jill as she addressed leadership issues and problems of change management. We watched as she found what worked and discussed why, and explored why the same approach could not be applied universally in all situations. We listened to her thoughts on leadership, what it was, how she led and where that matched what she was reading. Why she disagreed in some instances. Together we explored past experiences – the hard job of learning to lead by example, letting people free to have authority for decisions and actions. Developing staff who were nervous of decision-making roles (and then supporting or helping them before it got out of hand).

The other area was the need to make decisions on acceptable levels of risk, risk for staff, or for patients or indeed the Trust. All had to be articulated, explored and considered. As a result Jill took the lead in some developments in the Trust-wide risk process. Our debates also influenced my thinking as I tried to move the Trust from reactive risk management to a more proactive approach.

This was for me a very positive approach to learning. In the past many of the nurses that I have encouraged, or pushed to study at degree level, have been depressed at the lack of understanding between practice and education. Many valid pieces of work sit on shelves, unable to be used in practice. This move to value work based learning gives professional pride and improves patient care – because it is live and real in the workplace and enables the student to apply theory to practice and *vice versa*.

Regretfully the many other senior nurses with whom I have worked and who have made enormous changes, developed roles and systems of patient care, have not had this practice recognised academically, even though they have taught others and shared practice within and without the Trust, thus advancing nursing practice. Jill has done all this, but because Northumbria University recognised work based learning, she has successfully used that as the basis to attain her degree at Masters level. At the same time we have demonstrated that everything a practitioner has learnt in practice can be recognised and accredited as part of the academic process of assessment.'

The role of being Jill's peer in practice was earlier defined as a professional facilitator, a sounding board to explore ideas while also being able to help move the project along by opening avenues and helping legitimise aspects of the project. Margaret's account certainly does reflect what is expected from such a role. In fact without such peer support the whole of the learning experience could well become detached from the practice initiative.

With Jill leading the Patient Focused Care initiative and Margaret being the Director of Nursing and professional facilitator within the tripartite learning contract, the educational support was John's responsibility.

John:

'Tripartite learning contracts certainly seem to be a very productive way of learning collaboratively. Meeting with Jill and Margaret at Shotley Bridge Hospital in the first of what turned out to be several contract meetings was quite an adventure for myself. The theme for Jill's three practice projects was Patient Focused Care. Everything seemed ready for change. A new hospital was being built and a new model of care agreed. In many respects the practice projects were equally as new. As the educationalist in the contract I appreciated that Jill would want to know from me, if what she was doing reflected Masters level outcomes.

We already had the module outcomes for each practice project. When Jill undertook the MA Advanced Practice the objective was to address two characteristics of advanced practice within each practice project. For Practice Project One, there was assessment and risk as well as the advancement of nursing skills, for Practice Project Two there was empowerment and leadership and for Practice Project Three, change and evaluation. Although we planned a series of tripartite contract meetings over two semesters we still had to agree on how we would conduct out meetings. It was important that the practice initiative, Patient Focused Care drove the development.

We agreed at our first tripartite meeting an overarching plan for all three practice projects. What we wanted to avoid was the possibility of being distracted from the project by focusing too much on the characteristics of advanced practice or the module outcomes. Having agreed an action plan for each practice project we believed that by adhering to the plans we would also meet al.l the module and characteristic outcomes. This soon became a reality at our subsequent contract meetings. As Jill gave feedback about how the PFC initiative was unfolding we could see quite clearly relationships between actions she had undertaken, the module outcomes and more specifically the characteristics of advanced practice identified within the MA Advanced Practice programme.

At tripartite learning contract meetings Jill was able to reflect upon all the different activities she had undertaken. The interesting aspect to this reflection was how easily her decision-making and problem-solving fitted either explicitly or in the early stages implicitly into the characteristics. Initially she had to assess her practice situation and consider what risks could be taken. As the project developed there were issues of empowerment and leadership constantly being raised while in the final stages Jill looked upon the whole development from a change context as well as the issues of implementing and evaluating outcomes.

It was important to loosely work along the circular process of action research (Lewin, 1946) in that Jill was planning activities, implementing them, then fact-finding for evaluation. It is equally important to remember the potential ethical implications when fact-finding. The tripartite learning contract meetings were useful in clarifying how data was to be collected to evaluate certain aspects of the project and whether ethical approval would be necessary.

What Jill did in all the meetings was relate much of what was happening while introducing PFC to various taught components of the MA programme. She was able to link much of her project management to knowledge she had gleaned from modules on critical thinking, decision-making, risk, clinical assessment and change. What frequently happened in discussion were almost transient reflective experiences when Jill would make sense of something by referring to discussions she had had in a particular taught teaching session.

The practice projects had to be reflective but also had to demonstrate that the competence needed to achieve a particular characteristic or module outcome could be shown through the inclusion of evidence. We initially had some lengthy discussions on what could constitute evidence and as time progressed it was Jill who would turn up at meetings with relationships identified between evidence and outcomes.

What seemed different and far more interesting from this sequence of three practice projects as opposed to a traditional empirical research study was the extent to which this had become a living experience. Jill's project was certainly going to influence the way so many practitioners worked. But more importantly everyone felt part of what was happening. Those who knew Jill knew she was leading the Patient Focused Care initiative but also knew she was using it as her project for a Masters programme of study.

As Jill successfully passed Practice Project One and Two, her confidence grew. Her ability to manage the whole project was impressive. She still had her own apprehensions, especially when co-ordinating activities across professional boundaries and demonstrated much sensitivity as well as assertiveness in moving the project forward. It was following meetings she had with other professional groups that it became apparent how competent she had become in managing such a complex project. Confrontations with Doctors, Physiotherapists and Occupational Therapists in arriving at common agreement did become frequent and although progress was not always as Jill had planned, her negotiation skills were commendable.

It was apparent at the tripartite learning contract meetings that Jill was leading the PFC initiative, while managing our meetings to ensure she met the outcomes of the MA Advanced Practice programme. Over the three projects she empowered people, facilitated new learning as well as demonstrated growth in her own leadership and professional development. She brought about substantive change in practice, gained the respect of her colleagues across different professions and contributed to the understanding Northumbria University has of tripartite learning contracts. Her eventual evaluation of the project influenced hospital policy to the extent that PFC became the accepted model of patient management.

> It has been suggested that the educationalists role in such contracts is collaborative, moving from didactic to facilitative – teaching role. My perception does reflect this as I felt our contract meetings were sharing and flexible to ensure that the practice development was always the main focus of our meetings.'

Having set out to discuss the work based learning that arose within a tripartite learning contract, it has become quite evident that the work based learning that Jill undertook while implementing PFC was certainly not the only learning that was happening. The benefit of Jill, Margaret and John collaborating within the tripartite learning contract meant that each party could make their own contribution while also benefiting from each other's knowledge and experience.

John's role was primarily to encourage Jill to meet the criteria of her action plan and link what was happening in the project to outcomes identified within the characteristics of advanced practice. It was important to see that such a role can only be fulfilled if educationalists move towards a facilitative and learning style of collaboration. What is equally important is how Margaret saw her role, in making the contract viable and meaningful, while giving Jill support at a personal as well as professional level. Margaret's objective of helping to transfer Jill's learning into the Trusts working groups and *vice versa* does reflect the diverse and flexible nature of learning in such situations and highlights the benefits of true collaborative working. As an assessment methodology, the benefits for Jill were evident. Throughout the tripartite learning contract meetings there was considerable diagnostic help, while by the time each of the three projects were complete, both Margaret and John had 'lived the experience' with Jill.

The practice projects are certainly making a major contribution to work based learning within academic programmes run by Northumbria University. Recent developments have seen new practice project modules established which attract 60 credits at Masters level and are viewed in the same way empirical and systematic studies are.

References

Allan, D. and Cornes, D. (1998) 'The impact of management of change projects on practice: a description of the contribution that one educational programme made to the quality of health care.' *Journal of Advanced Nursing* 27(4) pp. 865–869.

Allen, A. (1993) 'Changing theory in nursing practice.' *Senior Nurse* 13 (1) pp. 43–45.

Booze-Allen, Hamilton (1988) 'Operational Restructuring. A recipe for success.' *Health Care Viewpoint* (Booz-Allen Hamilton, London).

Boud, D., Keogh, R. and Walker, D. (1985) *Reflection: Turning Experience into learning* (Nichols, New York).

Bowling, A. (1992) 'Assessing health needs and measuring patient satisfaction.' *Nursing Times Occasional Paper* 88 (31) pp. 31–34.

Brider, P. (1992) 'The move to Patient Focused Care.' *American Journal of Nursing* 6 (5) pp. 26–33.

Bruffee, K.A. (1987) 'The Art of Collaborative Learning. Making the most of knowledge peers.' *Change* 2 (19) pp. 45–47.

Cahill, J. (1995) 'Innovation and role of the change agent.' *Professional Nurse* 11 (1) pp. 57–58.

Deggerhammer, M. and Wade, B. (1991) 'The introduction of a new system of care delivery into a surgical ward in Sweden.' *International Journal of Nursing Studies* 28 (4) pp. 325–336.

Department of Health (1997) *The New NHS: Modern Dependable* (Cmnd 3807 HMSO, London).

Department of Health (1998) *A First Class Service* (DoH, London).

Devine, A. and Baxter, T. (1995) 'Introducing clinical supervision: a guide.' *Nursing Standard* 9 (40) pp. 32–34.

Dimond, B. (1995) *Legal Aspects of Nursing* (2nd edn) (Prentice Hall, London).

Doerge, J. and Hagenhowe, N. (1995) 'Management Restructuring. Toward a leaner organisation.' *Nursing Management* 26 pp. 32–38.

Dowling, S., Barrett, S. and West, R. (1995) 'With nurse practitioners, who needs house officers?' *British Medical Journal* 311 pp. 309–313.

Eubanks, P. (1991) 'Restructuring Care: patient focus is key to innovation.' *Hospitals* 5 pp. 25–26.

Ford, S. (1997) 'Change? No problem.' *Nursing Management* 4 (5) pp. 12–14.

French, J.R.P. and Raven, B.H. (1959) *The basis of social power* in Kagan, C. and Evans, J. (ed) (1995) *Professional Interpersonal Skills for Nurses* pp. 182 (Chapman & Hall).

Garside, P. (1993) *Patient Focused Care. A Review of Seven Sites in England* (NHS Management Executive, Leeds).

Gokhale, A. (1999) *Collaborative Learning Enhances Critical Thinking.* Digital library and Archives. http://scholar.llb.vt.edu/edu/ejournals

Grohar-Murray. M.E. and DiCroce, H.R. (1997) *Leadership & Management in Nursing* (2nd edn) (Appleton & Lange, Stamford).

Hart, E. (1996) 'Action research as a professionalising strategy: issues and dilemmas.' *Journal of Advanced Nursing* 23 (3) pp. 454–461.

Hart, E. and Bond, M. (1995) *Action Research for Health and Social Care* (Open University Press, Milton Keynes).

Heyman, T.D. and Culling, W. (1994) *The patient focused approach: a better way to run a hospital?* (Kingston Hospital NHS Trust, Kingston Upon Thames).

Holloway, I. and Wheeler, S. (1996) *Qualitative Research for Nurses* (Blackwell Science).

Holter, I. and Schwartz-Barcott, D. (1993) 'Action Research. What is it? How has it been used and how can it be used in nursing?' *Journal of Advanced Nursing* (18) pp. 298–304.

Hurst, K. (1995) *Progress with Patient Focused Care in the United Kingdom* (NHS Executive).

Jarvis, P. (1992) 'Reflective practice and nursing.' *Nurse Education Today* (12) pp. 174–181.

Johns (1995) 'The value of reflective practice for nursing.' *Journal of Clinical Nursing* (4) pp. 23–30.

Johns, C. (1995) 'Framing learning through reflection within Carpers Fundamental ways of knowing.' *Journal of Advanced Nursing* (22) pp. 226–234.

Johns, C. (1993) *Guided reflection* in Palmer, A., Burns, S. and Bulman, C. (1995) *Reflective Practice in Nursing. The Growth of the Professional Practitioner* (Blackwell Science, London).

Kitson, A. (1999) 'The essence of nursing.' *Nursing Standard* 13 (24) pp. 34–36.

Kouzes, J. and Posner, B. (1997) *The leadership challenge* (Jossey-Bass, San Francisco).

Lancaster, J. (1999) *Nursing Issues in Leading and Managing Change* (Mosby, St Louis).

Layton, A. (1993) 'Planning individual care with protocols.' *Nursing Standard* 8 (1) pp. 32–34.

Leifers, D. (1996) 'Trusting in Leadership.' *Nursing Standard* 10 (47) pp. 14.

Leonard, S. (1999) 'The expanded role of the registered nurse: studying nurses perceptions.' *Nursing Standard* 13 (43) pp. 14–20.

Lewin, K. (1946) 'Action Research and Minority Problems.' *Journal of Social Issues* (2) pp. 34–46.

Lewin, K. (1951) *Field Theory in Social Science* (Harper and Row, New York).

Liedkta, J. and Whitten, E. (1996) 'Building Better Patient Care Services: A Collaborative Approach.' *Health Care Management Review* 22 (3) pp. 16–24.

MacGregor (1990) 'Collaborative Learning; Shared Inquiry as a Process for Reform.' *New Directions for Teaching and Learning*. No.42 (Summer) pp. 19–31.

Maggenis, C., Slevin, E. and Cunningham, J. (1999) 'Nurses attitudes to the extension and expansion of their clinical role.' *Nursing Standard* 13 (51) pp. 8–14.

May, C. (1997) 'The professional imagination: narrative and the symbolic boundaries between medicine and nursing.' *Journal of Advanced Nursing* pp. 1094–1100.

McKinley, J. (1980) *Group Development through Participation Training* (Paulist Press, New York).

McKinley, J. (1983) 'Training for Effective Collaborative learning.' *New Directions for Continuing Education* (19) pp. 13–22.

Meyer, J.E. (1993) 'New Paradigm Research in Practice: the trials and tribulations of action research.' *Journal of Advanced Nursing* (18) pp. 1,066–1,072.

Minnen, T.G., Berger, E., Ames, A., Dubree, A., Baker, W.L. and Spinella, J. (1993) 'Sustaining work redesign innovations through shared governance.' *Journal of Nursing Administration* 23 (7/8) pp. 35–40.

Morgan, G. (1993) 'The implications of Patient Focused Care.' *Nursing Standard* 7 (52) pp. 37–39.

National Committee of Inquiry into Higher Education (1997) *National Committee of Inquiry into Higher Education Report* (Chair Sir Ron Dearing) (Newcombe House, London).

Newton, C. (1995) 'Action Research: application in practice.' *Nurse Researcher* 2 (3) pp. 60–71.

O'Brian, Y.M. and Stepura, B.A. (1992) 'Designing roles for assistive personnel in a rural hospital.' *Journal of Nursing Administration* 22 (10) pp. 34–37.

Ovretveit, J. (1998) *Evaluating Health Care* (Open University Press, Buckingham).

Parahoo, K. (1997) *Nursing Research. Principles, Process and Issues* (Macmillan, London).

Parker, S. and Wilson, C. (1992) *An Introduction to Medico-Legal Aspects of Practice Nursing* (Medical Defense Union, London).

Philips, C., Palfrey, C. and Thomas, P. (1994) *Evaluating Health & Social Care* (Macmillan, London).

Porter, and O'Grady, T. (1993) 'Patient Focused Care service models and nursing: perils and possibilities'. *Journal of Nursing Administration* 23 (3) pp. 7–8,15.

Powell, J.H. (1989) 'The reflective practitioner in nursing.' *Journal of Advanced Nursing* (14) pp. 824–832.

Prochaska, J.O., CiClemente, C.C. and Norcross, J.C. (1992) 'In Search of How People Change.' *American Psychologist* 47 (9) pp. 1,102–1,114.

Redman, R. and Jones, K. (1998) 'Effects of Implementing Patient Centred Care Models on Nurse and Non-Nurse Managers.' *Journal of Nursing Administration* 28 (11) pp. 46–53.

Robson C. (1997) *Real World Research* (Blackwell, Oxford).

Rogers, E. and Schoemaker, F. (1971) *Communication of Innovations: A Cross Cultural Approach* in Lancaster, J. (ed) (1999) *Nursing Issues in Leading and Managing Change* (Mosby, St Louis).

Roth, T. (1998) 'Patient Satisfaction: The Survey says...' *Nursing Case Management* 3 (5) pp. 184–191.

Routh, B.A. and Stafford, R. (1996) 'Implementing a Patient Focused Care Delivery Model.' *Journal of Nursing Staff Development* 12 (4) pp. 208–212.

Schon, D.A. (1987) *Educating the reflective practitioner* (Jossey-Bass, San Francisco).

Smith, A. and Russell, J. (1991) 'Using critical learning incidents in nurse education.' *Nurse Education Today* 11 pp. 284–291.

Southwick, K. (1993) 'Patient Focused Care on a tight budget prepares two hospitals for continued success in captivation environment.' *Strategies for Health Care Excellence* 6 (9) pp. 1–9.

Sullivan, E.J. and Decker, P.J. (1997) *Effective Leadership & Management in Nursing* (Addison Wesley, California).

Tingle, J. (1995) 'Clinical protocols and the law.' *Nursing Times* 91 (29) pp. 27–28.

Totten, S. (1991) *Co-operative Learning; a Guide to Research* (Garland, New York).

United Kingdom Central Council (1992) *Code of Professional Conduct* (3rd edn) (UKCC, London).

Webb, C. (1991) *Action Research in The Research Process in Nursing* (2nd edn) (ed D.F.S. Cormack), (Blackwell Science, Oxford) pp. 15–165

Wilson, J. (1997) *Integrated Care Management: the Path to Success* (Butterworth Heinmann).

Chapter 10

Education for multi-professional working

Maggie Coates and Andrew Mellon

Introduction

The purpose of this chapter is to discuss the issue of education in relation to multi-professional working. Several areas will be discussed within the context of changing health professional roles to demonstrate how educational opportunities can provide a catalyst for cross-fertilisation of ideas in relation to client care. The chapter is structured to enable the reader to ascertain how Higher Education linked to the clinical arena provided the opportunity for a generic community children's nurse to develop practice in partnership with a consultant paediatrician.

Section One outlines changes for both medical and nursing roles for the development of new services within the twenty-first century in relation to multi-professional practice, education and training. Section Two provides insight into the development of the practice project (paediatric gastrostomy assessment tool) from the clinical supervisors perspective, including key issues in relation to learning/tripartite contracts and learning needs. Section Three provides a more reflective account of the supervisee's experiences.

Section One

Setting the scene – a context for multi-professional working

There are huge challenges with the development of new services in the NHS at the start of the twenty-first century. Delivery of care is central to many of these changes and the role of the nurse and doctor in a modern health service is a topic for lively debate among fellow professionals, administrators and health care managers as well as the public and politicians. Charles West, the founder of Great Ormond Street Hospital for Children, and developer of nurse training at that institution wrote that,

> '... *the fact that medical men as a body advocate the training of nurses and teaching of midwives, and yet deprecate the practice of medicine by women is sometimes brought against them as an inconsistency... the requirements of the two are widely different, in one case a far shorter and less complete education than in the other. In the perfect nurse we require, first of all, a quality which is the especial attribute of a woman... the nurse needs an amount of technical skill which is gained by long practice, and which the doctor has no leisure to acquire... she must have knowledge enough of disease to carry out intelligently the directions she receives.*' (West, 1878, p. 28)

West's main distinction between those suited to be doctors and those suited to be nurses was based on gender, but he highlights a distinction in roles, which, is still pertinent today and reflected in some nursing opinion (Crowther, 2002).

Perhaps surprisingly major medical bodies in recent years have shown increasingly strong support for the development of nursing roles into what have been previously considered medical activities. The Royal College of Physicians recently published a working paper advocating a...

> '... *radical review of the role undertaken by all health professionals in order to implement a policy of skill mix and flexible working, designed to redistribute the ever-increasing workload and thus leaving doctors and nurses in a better position to apply their specific skills to management of patients. The expanded role of nurses across a range of clinical activities should be encouraged.*'
> (Orme *et al.* 2001)

There has been a rapid change in the roles that nursing staff have been asked to undertake. It is quite bewildering to many health professionals when faced with nursing colleagues sporting the title practitioners, specialists or consultants, as examples of three of the more common epithets. This also leads to confusion about how best to offer training to such individuals. It is not too surprising therefore that there has been such a profusion of courses offering training to nursing staff in such expanded roles.

This move towards more flexible approaches to care delivery has led to reviews of how best to deliver the training for such roles. Central guidance from the Department of Health has appeared in the form of policy documents firmly establishing the need for an adaptable, learning health service which is able to respond to the huge demands for change and development that are placed on it. At least three of its major aims impinge directly on the issues of multi-professional practice, education and training, namely teamworking across professional and organisational boundaries, maximising the contribution of all staff to patient care and modernising education and training to ensure that staff are equipped with the skills they need to work in a complex, changing NHS (DoH, 2000). The report of the Bristol Royal Infirmary Inquiry included among its recommendations; a need for 'shared learning across professional boundaries... the education, training and Continuing Professional Development (CPD) of all health care professionals should include joint courses between the professions. There should be more opportunities than at present for multi-professional teams to learn, train and develop together (London Stationery Office, 2001).

In our own area of work in paediatrics, multi-professional working has been a feature for a long time with health visitors working alongside general practitioners and community paediatric staff. Recent years have seen an increase in the varied roles and responsibilities of nursing staff in child health. Over the 50 years since the inception of the NHS we have witnessed the rise of technological medicine. Survivors of prematurity and congenital diseases, which would until recently have proved fatal, are testament to our greater ability to offer care that simply was not feasible in the past. While for many children life is transformed, for many others care is an ongoing, often a lifelong issue, placing new pressures on the health service to address their needs.

These developments in turn require more sophisticated systems of care with more advanced skills than would have been expected of health professionals of all types even 20 years ago. The role of the nursing profession in the delivery of paediatric and child health services is presently a hugely important issue both at the level of providing specialist care that has arisen with the development of tertiary specialties such as renal medicine, cardiology and oncology and the need to deliver some aspects of care that have traditionally been the domain of junior doctors. Expanded roles have developed in some areas of paediatric practice quicker than others, for example, neonatology, although, the perception of the paediatric medical profession has not always been positive about such developments (Hale *et al.* 1987).

In terms of learning, these new pressures to increase the range of tasks performed by professional groups result in an increase in the need to cross-traditional inter-professional boundaries and increasingly to look to shared learning experiences for professionals, with different roles within multidisciplinary teams. This multi-professional education may be defined as 'a learning process in which people from different professional backgrounds learn together.' Alongside this,

Inter-Professional Education (IPE) during which members of more than one health and/or social care profession learn interactively together, for the purpose of improving collaborative practice and/or the health/well being of patients/clients has become a subject of much study and reflection. During a systematic review of the Cochrane Database 1042 abstracts looked at studies into the effectiveness of IPE. The review found 'no conclusive evidence of the effectiveness of IPE in relation to professional practice and/or health care outcomes.' Although work is continuing to try and assess the impact of such educational interventions this is outside the scope of this chapter. However, in terms of the cross-fertilisation of ideas between two different health professionals in this particular case, Section Two goes on to explore general issues highlighted in relation to multi-professional and inter-professional working.

Section Two

Supervisors perspective – multi-professional and inter-professional issues: a practice project for the development of a paediatric gastrostomy assessment tool

A great deal is written about the adult learner that could equally relate to the supervision of adult learning activities. In general, supervisors are interested in the process of learning and hopefully find the process a dynamic one that acts to stimulate them as much as the student. Our experience was based around a tripartite learning contract between student, academic supervisor and clinical supervisor. There are a number of potential benefits and drawbacks to this approach. Ostensibly the role of an academic supervisor was to focus on the academic nursing resources that were available to the student, while the clinical supervisor was in the workplace and had a greater knowledge of the student's working environment. Doubling the supervision provides a greater opportunity to generate ideas, discuss issues, offer constructive criticism and assess progress.

The academic supervisor has knowledge of the course and overall standards, which was useful as a guide not only to the supervisee but also to the clinical supervisor. The clinical supervisor was able to offer knowledge and expertise within the paediatric field in support of both the clinical assessment module (Appendix) and the practice project. This helped to inform discussion between academic supervisor and supervisee. One important aspect of this was to ensure that theoretical considerations did not lead to impractical suggestions of how the project designed around the development of an assessment tool for children's gastrostomy sites proceeded, whilst simultaneously ensuring that theoretical key characteristics of the project could be met. This mechanism would have allowed for early detection of any potential problems that could have arisen in relation to the process of translation of academia into actual practice. A potential difficulty for many students enrolling on Higher Education (HE) courses is understanding new language. Although, adult learners have been described as being motivated and self-directed in their outlook (Knowles, 1990) it is perhaps easy to forget when putting together course material that the supervisee at entry to the course is different in their level of sophistication from the supervisee at completion.

Written information is frequently an early point of contact a student has with the course and its presentation may influence decisions about enrolment or have a significant effect to motivate or de-motivate the new student. Highly technical language, which relies heavily on the jargon of educationalists or 'experts' can deter the learning process especially when referring to assessment criteria. Interpretation or acknowledgement of the lack of clarity of such material is an important role for the supervisor. Our experience highlighted that language that might seem clear to a course organiser was a significant cause of concern. On this occasion, the end result from the course didn't relate to the ability of the trainee to understand course material at this early stage. However, course material that serves to prevent a student completing work and assignments to their highest standard could serve to detract from the designated area of study, and act as a confounding factor in their assessment.

This highlights a valuable role for the academic supervisor if the clinical supervisor is inexperienced either in terms of supervision generally or with the requirements of the course in particular. Experience in other settings has demonstrated the anxiety that supervisors feel when undertaking the role for a specific course for the first time. Success for the supervisee is extremely helpful in subsequent supervision on the same course. It allows for greater confidence in the provision of guidance not only in the requirements but also in helping them gauge the standard expected of them. This depends on the supervisor supervising a successful candidate. Conversely a student who does not achieve what they expect is often a cause for anxiety on the part of the supervisor, that they have in some way failed the student, and this can be very demoralising if it occurs without support from course organisers.

It is intriguing that experience in supervision in one setting seems to transpose itself quite well to different supervisory roles. Irrespective of the course content most postgraduate training programmes seem to be looking for similar qualities in successful supervisees. Not surprisingly, these quality descriptors can be lifted almost intact from any mainstream literature on adult education – self-direction, curiosity, attention to detail, reflection, progression, linking common themes through a portfolio of work. What is often more difficult is putting across this concept to supervisees in a way that allows them to see the value of working in a staged manner to achieve their objectives by applying the principles of the course. Many students look at the long-term outcome expected and may be daunted when faced with the ultimate standard as their key objective. Courses with clear objectives designed to encourage the student to work in a structured manner are very helpful. In this case the practice project was built up in a structured way from the theoretical considerations through to its implementation in clinical practice.

However, supervision of individual nurses undertaking HE is not a role that medical training prepares a doctor for. Nursing education seems to have been quicker to recognise the value of training in educational supervision with qualifications in preceptorship commonly found among trained staff. In the medical profession there have been increasing calls on senior medical staff to supervise various areas of the training activity of junior doctors in particular, and more frequently supervising the educational activities of nursing professionals and others in the clinical field. For many doctors, supervision is first encountered during a period of research undertaken while in training grade posts (Senior House Officer, Specialist Registrar) with a view to obtaining a higher degree. Until recently their own experience of having been supervised as a student might be the only example a doctor had before undertaking supervision of a student. Recently, however, training for the educational supervision of junior doctors has been introduced, which encompasses educational planning, assessment of performance and appraisal aimed at learner centred review and feedback.

Additionally, there are increasing numbers of more formal qualifications available from highly focused short courses such as the advanced life support courses to courses delivered over a year or more such as Certificates and Diplomas in Medical Education and Masters of Medical Science that have developed to address specific training needs. Within nursing in our own and nearby Trusts there are clinical skills courses for nurse practitioners in adult specialties, neonatal nurse practitioner training courses, courses for training nurses in high dependency care, degree level and Masters level courses in clinical practice, all of which cater for different groups of learners. This highlights that supervision is an increasing component required of both senior medical and nursing staff. Different facets of the supervisory role may be developed as the individual takes on new roles – examples include training in educational supervision for junior doctors, communication skills training, medical education and Royal College activities training.

There are assumptions in some quarters that adult learners should be able to work without support, however, medical schools and universities are increasingly formalising supervision arrangements for medical trainees enrolled for higher qualifications such as an MD or PhD, as it becomes more important for departments to demonstrate their research success as part of the Research Assessment Exercise periodically undertaken in all British university departments. The research grading has become such a crucial part of the method by which universities attract funding that it is no longer simply the 'supervisee' who has a vested interest in their own success. Educationally the value of the supervisee-supervisor relationship has perhaps been underestimated and it is interesting to see economic practicalities causing changes in practice.

Whatever conceptual framework underpins supervision there appears to be four key elements needed to increase the probability of success in a given project such as this one – a motivated student, an appropriate project, secure funding and good supervision. The role of the supervisor gradually develops and is influenced by the various experiences and training opportunities that present themselves during a professional career. There has often been more of a focus on the requirements of students – entry characteristics, expected workload and assessment strategies – rather than the individual taking on the role of supervisor, this appears to occur more by chance than planning as a need arises. Assessment of supervisors' skills and CPD should perhaps be given a higher profile when educational events and training courses are planned. This does occur in some contexts, and can be reflected most overtly from personal experience in life support courses, where responsibility for instructor training is maintained by the same organisations that run the life support training.

Generally, involvement in supervision of both medical and nursing trainees in a number of settings suggests that many of the issues that arise in training for a multi-professional role in paediatric practice are common to most adult learners undertaking further formal training on an HE course. It is only human nature to look for shortcuts and the pressure of time on many postgraduate students can lead them to underestimate the time requirements of a particular course. Clearly, deadlines are an important motivating factor as is the need for a supervisor to ensure that the student has a realistic understanding of the time required to complete a piece of work. Working to a tight deadline is feasible if preparatory work has been done at an earlier stage. Encouragement to students that following the guidance provided is the way to achieve success is vital and that education is a journey of experience not simply an exercise in arriving at the destination on time.

With this in mind, the development of a tool for clinical assessment of gastrostomy sites was evolutionary as it followed our working experience in dealing with these problems on a daily basis. Although, problems with gastrostomies are relatively common they were often addressed independently by a medical specialist or community children's nurse, this resulted in a loss of training opportunities for more junior staff, both nursing and medical.

Problems arose when neither was immediately available and this sometimes led to delays in instituting appropriate treatment or inappropriate treatment being started. In terms of multi-professional working, this offered a good example of a situation in which more than one group of health professionals might be involved in delivering the same care and that the care given might be influenced by the background of that caregiver. There were a small number of common interventions required that could be simplified by the development of a structured guideline – paediatric gastrostomy assessment tool. The few important complications that need to be distinguished could also be managed within the same guideline. Experience of problems from a medical and nursing perspective was an important part of the process as there are some facets of gastrostomy care that require a more urgent intervention and tended to present to medical teams, but other common problems which were commonly seen by the community nursing team and rarely presented to the medical team.

A key clinical supervisory role for the development of the tool was helped by a cycle of discussion, reflection and remodelling until it was felt that the key questions we as experienced practitioners were asked about gastrostomy sites had been dealt with within the assessment tool. Section Three goes on to outline these processes in the context of the supervisor and supervisee relationship from the supervisee's perspective in more depth using a reflective approach.

Section Three

The supervisee's perspective – a reflective account of a generic community children's nurse developing practice in partnership with a consultant paediatrician

The appointment into a new post as a generic community children's nurse and the commencement of the MA in Advanced Practice (Nursing) is the basis for the examination of a multi-professional working partnership between a consultant paediatrician and a nurse developing practice. Within the MA Advanced Practice (Nursing) the traditional dissertation is replaced with a practice project that spans the two-year pathway and includes achievement of key characteristics. As a Community Children's Nurse, the practice project involved the development of a gastrostomy assessment tool for children that could be utilised within the multi-professional team. In order for key characteristics to be met, and within the traditional tripartite mechanism for learning it was necessary to select a clinical supervisor that would enable the process of the practice project to be supported.

The exploration of the relationship between the supervisor and supervisee in this instance may determine key concepts that led to its success expose some of the reflective notions of the supervisee and identify possible teaching and learning strategies adopted. Although, the focus for this discussion centres on the relationship between two of the individuals involved (supervisor and supervisee) within true tripartite style the academic supervisor is formally acknowledged as having a similarly valuable role in facilitating development of critical theory borne out of self-reflection and in terms of self-development.

One can only make assumptions in relation to the rationale of any supervisor agreeing to undertake a role such as this. In this case, the supervisee's assumption is based on the premise of social exchange theory (Hale, 2000) and the knowledge that there would be at some point an element of return benefit. With regard to the supervisee, the attraction of the supervisoring relationship centred on the belief in the ability of the supervisor to adopt the primary role necessary for completion of the course; the provision of a learning experience and environment from a social constructionist perspective (Shotter, 1993; Gergen 1994). Through interaction, new understandings and realties would be constructed (Rix & Gold, 2000). Additionally, the personal characteristics of the supervisor were valued, as highlighted by Darling (1984). Within Darling's Measuring Supervisor Potential Instrument (MSPI) these included mutual attraction, mutual respect and subscription of time and energy. However, Darling's instrument has not been widely utilised with only limited studies demonstrating its validity in terms of determining the important prerequisites of a good supervisor (Andrews, 1999).

During, what I have since determined as the introductory critical stage of the supervisor-supervisee relationship several factors were influential in determining how successful the relationship would become. Alongside the development of a new post came the workload and demands of the MA Advanced Practice (Nursing). Accompanying this was the sudden realisation that I was required to identify with, learn from and make sense of my past experience by the re-integration of existing knowledge with new knowledge. This included learning to function at an expert level within an unfamiliar environment through hands-on experience whilst meeting the demands of Masters level study. Although this was a generic community children's nursing post, a gap in service provision highlighted a need for a degree of specialist knowledge in an area of gastroenterology. To add focus, the practice project was specifically manufactured to increase clinical expertise in this specialist area in terms of problematic gastrostomies as well as the expertise of other clinicians caring for the client group. If I was to function at a level that would provide a quality service for the children who required care within this speciality I would need to increase a variety of skills, identify learning needs and determine how I could meet those needs.

In order to explore these learning needs, the notion of 'novice versus expert' (Benner, 1984) requires further examination to expose the reflective components of the experience. As a consequence of the transferable skills associated with several years of children's nursing and within Benner's (1984) conceptual framework 'From Novice to Expert' I was expected to be a proficient and expert practitioner. With a wealth of knowledge and skills caring for children I considered myself to be a competent and autonomous practitioner, fulfilling the prerequisites described by Thibodeau and Hawkins (1994) as contributing to advanced practice. These included advanced education, substantial knowledge base and the proficient use and application of that knowledge to promote all round excellence of practice (Thibodeau, 1994). Suddenly, I had to practice as the expert, making expert decisions in a specialist area of gastroenterology where I considered myself more of a novice. Perhaps, the notion of novice may have been a result of the recognition that current practice was based, not on the development of my own experiential evidence, clinical guidelines or search for the best possible evidence, but on *ad hoc* teaching and learning within the clinical arena by the consultant paediatrician.

As a result of the situation, excellent working relationships were developed. In essence, this informal, unassigned supervisor relationship, based on coaching in the clinical field and established on professional trust and teamwork became a formally structured partnership of supervisor and supervisee under the learning contract of the Masters process. This partnership would be influenced not only by the intention to change nursing practice, cross traditional boundaries of clinical assessment, diagnosis and management but also by the professional relationship between myself and those involved in the self-led tripartite learning contract. When the notion of advanced practice and the development of the practice project were in the primary stages, the model adapted was perhaps based on a traditional master/apprentice relationship (Hay, 1995) derived from a more behaviourist approach to learning (Thorndike, 1931; Skinner, 1971). However, this approach used in conjunction with effective support from the supervisor significantly increased the ability to adjust to this unfamiliar clinical setting (Spouse, 1998).

The initial notion of master/apprentice did foster elements of cognitive dissonance as a result of a firm personal belief in the ability of nurses to master the necessary skills and display the attributes to lead practice and contribute effectively to the demands of the clinical arena. In the event that several elements of this advancing role were carried out under the supervision of the consultant paediatrician who I had subsequently selected to be my supervisor I questioned whether I had negotiated or considered who had influence over my professional development within this new area of practice. I was conscious of the need to maintain emphasis on clear direction and enthusiasm to provide a quality nurse-led service with vision, excellence and pride (Bass, 1985) rather than fulfilling the work previously carried out by a medical practitioner. I was challenged to rethink old ways of doing things and to provide a flow of new ideas.

At this stage, the supervisory relationship had progressed from the earlier notion of master/apprentice (Hay, 1995) towards a more equal, interdependent and harmonious one. However, in the absence of formal interventionist methods for supervisor selection the notion of teaching and learning styles were never discussed. On reflection, having an awareness of these were crucial in determining strategies that would enable me to adopt the most effective methods to be able develop an advancing role, engineer cross-fertilisation of ideas and work multi-professionally towards the development of the gastrostomy assessment tool which was one of the predetermined learning outcomes.

As a reflector and a pragmatist (Honey & Mumford, 1982) with a natural tendency to be cautious, having the time to review and reflect on my experiences, in relation to the development of the practice project was valued. This reflective nature for learning was further facilitated by opportunities for observing my supervisor's expert practice within the clinical arena during joint home visits and clinic consultations. The ability to jointly review experiences was then utilised to generate alternative ways of working to benefit the client group by utilising and sharing thought processes, problem-solving and working in partnership to address any issues that presented. This discourse promoted a form of naturalistic enquiry (Lincoln & Guba, 1985) through seeking other individual points of view in relation to the context and realities of practice. It provided protection against surreptitious intrusion of our beliefs and values with regard to the nature and *raison d'être* of our given professions and the ownership of the practice project in terms of it remaining nurse-led.

In the process of developing the gastrostomy assessment tool and advancing practice, preferred learning styles were promoted by the supervisor based on encouragement of accuracy and a focus on the development of analytical skills, rather than just skill acquisition. This may have been the result of the working relationship, previously established between a doctor and a nurse, based on mutual respect, professional trust and teamwork, or the ability of the conceptual framework of the practice project to facilitate a two-way learning process between traditionally different practitioners. Additionally, it may have been a result of the unconscious nature of complimentary transactions. In terms of transactional analysis[1] (Berne, 1964) adult type behaviour prevailed which avoided crossed transactions during communication. The ability of both parties to hold open lines of communication was paramount. Although both supervisor and supervisee functioned in different roles the generality of the formulation of experiential knowledge (Benner, 1984) afforded the ability to determine behaviour mannerisms displayed to ascertain ego states.

Further focusing on communication, during the practical development of the gastrostomy assessment tool the supervisor acted as a sounding board to enable different perspectives to be considered. The facilitative nature of this was thought-provoking and encouraged the flow of ideas. A mutual interest based on the success of the practice project served to foster collegiality. In both parties striving to work collaboratively and adopt a sequential approach to gastrostomy assessment, the traditional 'barriers' associated within the context of medical power assertion were never an issue. Had medical power been asserted, then learning would have been more superficial as a result of a power imbalance, this may have adversely affected the learning experience (Beech & Brockbank, 1999). What replaced this was a supportive, humanistic relationship (Maslow, 1971; Rogers, 1969; Rogers & Freiburg, 1994) with encouragement and direction. To an observer this may have appeared a little *laissez-faire* in approach. In reality, this was dictated by workload constraints of the both parties. Often, these workload constraints produced feelings of guilt in terms of utilisation of the supervisor. As a result, any demands were kept to a minimum.

On reflection, this probably produced a more cohesive relationship in terms of the notion of a humanist learning environment (Maslow, 1908–1970; Rogers, 1969; Rogers & Freiburg, 1994) with supervisee learning styles complimented by minimal demands from the supervisor. The ability to achieve increasing autonomy and competence and meet key characteristics created a learning situation based on self-motivation, empowerment, self-direction (Tennant, 1997) and the desire to drive the practice project forward with a sense of freedom within the learning experience. Overall, these supervisor/supervisee characteristics within the relationship enabled the development of the link between theory and practice through what Hale describes as 'windows of insight' (Hale, 2000).

The reflective nature of the supervisee accompanied the ability for self-appraisal and knowledge development in relation to theory and practice. This was facilitated by the skill of the supervisor who provided valuable insights through windows of opportunity. These windows of opportunity were situated in the exposure of expertise of gastroenterology, initiation into the supervisor's views, experience and role within the organisation. As one of the key players, the ability of the supervisor to access the inner workings of the organisation further facilitated the development of the practice project.

This clearly demonstrated the supervisor's belief that the project was a worthwhile venture that should be strategically marketed and outwardly supported. A joint belief that I had the potential to succeed with the supervisor adopting a willing supportive role, without taking responsibility for decision-making (Grainger, 2002). Consistently, even in times when I was faced with self-doubt (Schon, 1987) and in 'the pit' of the change process (Manion, 1995) the supervisor encouraged the maintenance of motivation to meet the demands of the development of advanced practice through achievement of the key characteristics involved.

Within the conceptual framework of the MA Advanced Clinical Practice (Nursing) and the increasing development of clinical expertise the supervisory relationship moved from interdependence to independent in terms of knowledge acquisition whilst remaining facilitative of the process of the practice project. As the development of the gastrostomy assessment tool was nearing completion, the role of the supervisor was more evaluative in terms of the links between theory and practice. Through the necessary exploration of theory in relation to practice, this was demonstrated in the mastery of critical thinking skills and reasoning strategies in relation to the clinical practice of caring for children and families.

Further exploration of this highlights the concept of scaffolding (Wood *et al.* 1976; Spouse, 1998). Discussions based around the gastrostomy assessment tool, prompted exposure of the level of in-depth knowledge gained within the process as a whole. This included not only the epistemic knowledge and expertise (theory) gained within this new area of practice but also the transference of this epistemic knowledge into practical phronesis (practice). In cognitive terms this is conceptualised as movement through the Zone of Proximal Development, Vygotsky (1978) in order for theory and practice to be brought together (Spouse, 1998).

Within this stage of the learning experience, the development of metacognitive skills (Fonteyn & Cahill, 1998) conducive to sound critical thinking was necessary. A two-way questioning process between the supervisor and supervisee at a higher cognitive level demanded decisions about the accuracy and effectiveness of our assessment and interventions of care for the client group (Wink, 1993). Overall, this metacognitive awareness became more habitual in clinical practice. It was utilised when faced with a specific clinical problem whilst simultaneously identifying strategies for problem-solving. This equates with the ability to be reflexive within clinical practice rather than reflective. The ability to demonstrate autonomy by assuming the role of decision-maker and diagnostician harnessed these attributes in order to demonstrate skill acquisition and role transition (Fullbrook, 1998).

With the maintenance of the practice project remaining client-centred and the flexibility afforded by those supporting my efforts I was able to develop expert practice and specialisation firmly grounded in a children's nursing paradigm. However, the assumption that the gastrostomy assessment tool was a conscientious, explicit and judicious use of current best evidence (Sackett, 1997) remained a constant source of reflective concern. In relation to its use it was envisaged that it would be utilised by a variety of health professionals, with the aim of improving individual and group performance. In acknowledging these aims I had to be sure in the knowledge that clinical effectiveness was demonstrated. The crucial factor in this instance appears to be the notion of evidence based practice, which promoted much debate, analysis and critical thinking.

In adopting the gastrostomy assessment tool as evidence base *per se* there may be a danger of an inherent risk in subscribing to the albeit rather understandable assumption that the evidence utilised for the approach to assessment was in itself correct (Gordon, 1997). The ability of the supervisor to formulate and pose questions (Spouse, 1998) exposed the rationale for the way in which the tool was developed and the depth of detailed understanding of the clinical evidence upon which the gastrostomy assessment tool was based. The event that it was developed from a combined approach of experiential knowledge and skill from those with a vested interest rather than derived from theory, increased the status of empirical evidence by enabling the articulation of the epistemology of gastrostomy care in a meaningful and understandable language (Scholes, 1996). As a result small-scale projects such as this one could demonstrate value by producing evidence that can be validated and evaluated within the practitioner's own context (French, 1999).

Throughout this process, I have realised that there are many types of evidence aside from those that are given scientific credibility. These nursing empirics represent knowledge that I had found difficulty in establishing with reference to gastrostomy assessment. It was this knowledge that was seen as quantifiable, yielding objectivity and could be replicated (Carper, 1992). Both supervisor and supervisee envisaged that the gastrostomy assessment tool would be viewed in this way on completion. Based solely on empirical evidence, it may not have been perceived as one hundred percent accurate.

At this point, it seems pertinent to highlight that this non-empirical evidence (McKenna, 2000) upon which the gastrostomy assessment tool was developed was procured from the clinical practice of both paediatric medicine and nursing. It is conceptualised as a combination of prepositional knowledge (Schon, 1983) incorporated into practice whilst utilising my own growing experience within this context of care. The variability of the evidence base for this particular gastrostomy assessment tool ranged from my own developing hands-on expertise, or aesthetic knowledge as well as the experience of a trusted medical colleague. As an advancing practitioner I had the ability to establish and incorporate an informal cognitive database of evidence, which I could then utilise depending on the presenting problem. As a generator and translator of evidence (Humpherys, 1996) I was able to make judgements about recognising the good from the bad and know the strengths and weaknesses of the way in which gastrostomy stomas were assessed and treated.

It transpired that our own clinical experiences and expertise could constitute as evidence in the absence of research findings, as long as we remained professionally and personally accountable for our own actions (McKenna, 2000). What was required by us to guide the development of the gastrostomy assessment tool was the best evidence available to us at the time.

As a result, the reflective concern expressed earlier regarding the evidence base for the development of the gastrostomy assessment tool has been addressed, the evidence on which it is based, although not totally reliant on scientific credibility is multifaceted. This promotes a combination of factors designed to be flexible enough to meet the demands of individual children with complex care needs. It is envisaged that the evidence base would be continually evaluated using a combination of empirical and non-empirical evidence, inclusive of both professional judgement and experience to promote clinical decisions that are of benefit to the child and family. The gastrostomy assessment tool is not designed to replace these elements but to be utilised alongside them. It remains to be seen whether it is judged to be reliable enough to meet its objective – the provision of a structured assessment approach to children's gastrostomy stoma sites and subsequent improvements in the quality of care provision.

In providing reflections regarding the learning experience within the context of the MA Advanced Practice (Nursing) personal synthesis has been included. This revealed both the personal and professional growth achieved, inclusive of the way in which advanced practice skills have developed and contributed to clinical practice, within this, several critical stages conceptualised as being crucial to the overall process. It appears that the successful relationship between supervisor and supervisee may have been based exclusively on joint beliefs and values with several core concepts. A belief in the support for development of practice through education, for mutual respect and understanding of the differing roles of those involved and in the provision of a quality service for the client group based on available evidence and clinical experience. On reflection, the ability to link theory to practice became a catalyst for the exploration of any nuances within clinical practice, aided by the necessity to achieve the key characteristics outlined within the practice project.

Whatever the dynamics of the relationship, within the subsequent conducive learning environment I was able to independently adjust the boundaries of the role and meet the requirements of the practice project. In essence this worked well to benefit the client group and meet the key characteristics of the course. The ability to remain firmly entrenched within the conceptual framework of children's nursing was actively encouraged. The emphasis of the integration between theory and practice facilitated a myriad of benefits not only for clinical practice but also for the development of a more holistic understanding of the clinical experience as it relates to individual learning, self-reflection and self-awareness. This could then be related to the unique experience of caring for children and families. Perhaps it is this unique experience of caring for children and families that provided the cross-fertilisation of ideas in relation to the development of the practice project, alongside the ability of the supervisor to provide a challenge in relation to the quality of the work involved. This was of course accompanied by the ability of the supervisee to rise to that challenge in the final stages of the project.

Conclusion

Within this chapter several key areas have been discussed from both a general and reflective perspective focused on the process of clinical supervision within an HE conceptual framework. Within the context of the MA Advanced Practice (Nursing) an example of a small-scale project has highlighted the potential to improve the quality of care delivered by a number of health professionals for a specific client group. Since completion of the paediatric gastrostomy assessment tool, an inter-professional study is in progress to further evaluate its value, both as an assessment and management tool in its own right and as an educational tool for both medical and nursing staff. The context of this is now removed from the mechanism that created the initial development of the tool, however the cross-fertilisation of ideas is a continuous process. The learning process and the professional working relationship established between two health professionals from different backgrounds during this time enables this evaluative study to continue.

With respect to the ever-changing nature of clinical practice in both nursing and medicine dictated by the transforming needs of the client group and driven by the modernisation agenda of a NHS what remains to be seen is whether or not as individual groups of health professionals practicing alongside each other we can use the opportunities provided by increasing joint education, training and multi-professional working to meet the demands made by this twenty-first century care climate.

Note

1 Within Transactional Analysis the belief is that each individual has three ego states in action: The parent ego state, the adult ego state and the child ego state. Individuals are thought to adopt any one of these ego states at any one time and have a preference for one. It is the responder that chooses the ego- state to use within communication but this can depend on the stimulus provided by the other party. A stimulus originating in one persons child ego state frequently elicits the parent ego state in another (Jongeward & James, 1981).

References

Andrews, J. (1999) 'Supervision in nursing: a literature review.' *Journal of Advanced Nursing* 29 (1) pp. 201–207.

Bass, B.M. (1985) *Leadership and performance beyond expectations* (Free Press, New York). Cited in Rolfe, G. and Fullbrook, P. (1998) *Advanced Nursing Practice* (Butterworth and Heineman. Oxford). pp. 129.

Beech, Nic and Brockbank, A. (1999) 'Power, knowledge and psychosocial dynamics in supervisoring.' *Management Learning* 30 (1) pp. 7–25.

Benner, P. (1984) *From novice to expert.* (Addison Wesley, Menley Park. California).

Berne, E. (1964) *Transactional analysis in psychotherapy.* (Grove Press, New York) Cited in Ellis, R., Gates, R. and Kenworthy, N. (1995) *Interpersonal communication in nursing theory and practice* (Churchill, Livingstone).

Carper, B.A. (1992) *Philosophical inquiry in nursing: an application,* cited in McKenna, H. and McKenna, P. (2000) 'Evidence based practice: demolishing some myths.' *Nursing Standard.* 14 (16) pp. 39–42.

Crowther, M.A. (2002) *Why women should be nurses and not doctors.* Online UKCHN (www.qmuc.ac.uk/hn/history/seminars01.html).

Darling, L.A.W. (1984) 'What do nurses want in a supervisor?' *The Journal of Nursing Administration* October, pp. 42–44, cited in Andrews, J. (1999) 'Supervision in nursing: a literature review.' *Journal of Advanced Nursing.* 29 (1) pp. 201–207.

Department of Health. (2000) *A Health Service of all the talents: Developing the NHS workforce – Consultation Document on the Review of Workforce Planning,* p. 5.

Fonteyn, M. and Cahill, M. (1998) 'The use of clinical logs to improve nursing student's metacognition: a pilot study.' *Journal of Advanced Nursing* 28 (1) pp. 149–154.

French, P. 'The development of evidence based nursing.' *Journal of Advanced Nursing* 29 (1) January, pp. 72–78.

Fullbrook, P. (1998) *Advanced practice: the advanced practitioner perspective*, pp. 87–102, cited in Rolfe, G. and Fullbrook, P. (1998) *Advanced Nursing Practice* (Butterworth and Heineman, Oxford).

General Medical Council (2002) *Tomorrow's doctors: Recommendations on undergraduate medical education* (GMC).

Gergen, K.J. (1994) *Relationships and realities* (Harvard University Press, Boston) cited in Rix, M. and Gold, J. (2000) 'With a little help from my academic friend: supervising change agents.' *Supervising and Tutoring* 8 (1) p. 49.

Gordon, M. (1997) 'Questioning the evidence.' *Health Care Risk Report* December/January, pp. 18–19.

Grainger, C. (2002) *Supervising-supporting doctors at work and play* http://bmj.com/cgi/content/full/324/7353/S203 8/27/02.

Hale, P., Boxall, J. and Hunt, M. (1987) 'The role of the neonatal nurse practitioners: a viewpoint.' *Archives of Disease in Childhood* (62) pp. 760–761.

Hale, R. (2000) 'To match or mis-match? The dynamics of supervisoring as a route to personal and organisation learning.' *Continuous Professional Development Journal* (3) pp. 88–100.

Hay, J. (1995) *Transformational supervisoring.* (McGraw-Hill, London), cited in Hale, R. (2000) 'To match or mis-match? The dynamics of supervisoring as a route to personal and organisation learning.' *Continuous Professional Development Journal* (3) p. 92.

Honey, J. and Mumford, P. (1982) *The manual of learning styles* cited in Quinn, F.M. (2000) *The Principles and Practice of Nurse Education* (4th edn) (Stanley Thornes). pp. 35–36.

Humphreys, J. (1996) 'Old ideas, new jargon.' *Nursing Standard* 10 (16), cited in Rolfe, G. and Fullbrook, P. (1998) *Advanced Nursing Practice* (Butterworth and Heineman, Oxford).

Jongeward, D. and James, M. (1981) *Winning ways in health care – transactional analysis for effective communication* (Addison Wesley Publishing Company).

Knowles, M.S. (1990) *The Adult Learner: a neglected species* (4th edn) (Gulf Publishing, Houston) p.57.

Lincoln, Y.S. and Guba, E.G. (1985) *Naturalistic Inquiry* (Sage, London).

Mackway-Jones, K., Molyneux, E., Phillips, B. and Wieteska, S. (2001) *Advanced Paediatric Life Support: The Practical Approach* (3rd edn) (Advanced Life Support Group) (BMJ Books) Chapters 3, 8, 9, 10 and 11.

Manion, J. (1995) 'Understanding the seven stages of change.' *Journal of Advanced Nursing* (40) April, pp. 41–43.

Maslow, A, (1971) *The farther reaches of human nature* (Penquin, Hamondsmith) cited in Quinn, FM. (2000) *The Principles and Practice of Nurse Education* (4th edn) (Stanley Thornes) p. 19.

McKenna, H. and McKenna, P. (2000) 'Evidence based practice: demolishing some myths,' *Nursing Standard* 14 (16) pp. 39–42

Orme, M., Bloom, S. and Watkins, P. (2001) 'Skill mix in clinical care: prepared on behalf of the working party on skill mix by its chairman'. *Clinical Medicine. Journal of the Royal College of Physicians of London* 1 (4) pp. 259–260.

Rix, M. and Gold, J. (2000) 'With a little help from my academic friend: supervising change agents.' *Supervising and Tutoring* 8 (1) pp. 47–62.

Rogers, C. (1969) *Freedom to learn.* (Merrill, Ohio) cited in Quinn, FM (2000) *The Principles and Practice of Nurse Education* (4th edn) (Stanley Thornes) p. 53.

Rogers, C. and Freiberg, H.J. (1994) *Freedom to learn* (3rd edn) (Macmillian, New York) cited in Quinn, FM (2000) *The Principles and Practice of Nurse Education* (4th edn) (Stanley Thornes) p. 53.

Sackett, D. (1997) 'Evidenced based medicine: what is it and what isn't it?' *British Medical Journal* 312, pp. 71–72, cited in Mead, P. (1999) 'Clinical guidelines: promoting clinical effectiveness or a professional minefield?' *Journal of Advanced Nursing* 31 (1) pp. 110–116.

Scholes, J. (1996) 'Therapeutic use of self: how the critical care nurse uses self to the patients therapeutic benefit.' *Nursing Critical Care* 1 (2) pp. 60–65.

Schon, D. (1987) *Educating the reflective practitioner* (Jossey-Bass, San Francisco) cited in Atkins, S. and Murphy, K. (1993) 'Reflection: a review of the literature'. *Journal of Advanced Nursing* (18) pp. 1,188–1,192.

Schon, D. (1983) *The reflective practitioner. How professionals think in action.* (Temple Smith, London) cited in Hallet, C. (1997) 'Learning through reflection in the community: the relevance of Schon's theories of coaching to nurse education.' *International Journal of Nursing Studies* 34 (2) pp. 103–110.

Shotter, J. (1993) *Conversational realities* (Sage, London) cited in Rix, M. and Gold, J. (2000) 'With a little help from my academic friend: supervising change agents.' *Supervising and Tutoring* 8 (1) p. 49.

Skinner, B.F. (1971) *Beyond freedom and dignity* (Alfred Knopf, New York) cited in Quinn, F.M. (2000) *The Principles and Practice of Nurse Education* (4th edn). (Stanley Thornes) p. 14.

Spouse, J. (1998) 'Scaffolding student learning in clinical practice.' *Nurse Education Today* (18) pp. 259–266.

Spouse, J. (2001) 'Bridging theory and practice in the supervisory relationship: a socio-cultural perspective.' *Journal of Advanced Nursing* 33 (4) pp. 512–522.

Stationery Office (2001) *Learning from Bristol: the report of the public inquiry into children's heart surgery at The Bristol Royal Infirmary 1984–1995* (www.bristol-inquiry.org.uk/final-report/index.htm).

Tennant, M. (1997) *Psychology and adult learning.* (2nd edn) (Routledge, London) cited in Quinn, FM (2000) *The Principles and Practice of Nurse Education* (4th edn) (Stanley Thornes) p. 61.

Thibodeau, J. and Hawkins, J. (1994) 'Moving towards a nursing model in advanced practice.' *Western Journal of Nursing Research.* Vol. 16. pp. 205–218 cited in Dyson, L. (1997) 'Advanced nursing roles: their worth in nursing.' *Professional Nurse* 12 (10) pp. 728–732.

Thorndike, E. (1931) *Human Learning* (Appleton Century Crofts, New York) cited in Quinn, F.M. (2000) *The Principles and Practice of Nurse Education* (4th edn) (Stanley Thornes) p. 14.

Vygotsky, L.S. (1978) *Mind in society. The development of higher psychological processes* (Harvard University Press, Cambridge Mass) cited in Spouse, J. (2001) 'Bridging theory and practice in the supervisory relationship: a socio-cultural perspective.' *Journal of Advanced Nursing* 33 (4) p. 517.

West, C. (1878) *Medical women, a statement and an argument* (J. & A. Churchill, London) p. 28 cited in Crowther, MA. (2002) *Why Women should be Nurses and not Doctors* Online UKCHN (www.qmuc.ac.uk/hn/history/seminars01.html).

Wink, D.M. (1993) 'Using questioning as a teaching strategy.' *Nurse Educator*. Vol. 18. pp. 11–15 cited in Phillips, N. (2001) 'The questioning skills of clinical teachers and preceptors: a comparative study.' *Journal of Advanced Nursing* 33 (4) p. 528.

Wood, D., Brunner, J. and Ross, G. (1976) 'The role of tutoring in problem-solving.' *Journal of Child Psychology* Vol. 17 cited in Spouse, J. (2001) 'Bridging theory and practice in the supervisory relationship: a sociocultural perspective.' *Journal of Advanced Nursing* 33 (4) pp. 512–522.

Zwarenstein, M., Reeves, S., Barr, H., Hammick, M., Koppel, I. and Atkins, J. (2002) 'Inter-professional education: effects on professional practice and health care outcomes' (Cochrane Review) in *The Cochrane Library*, 4.

Part 3

The lessons learned from Accredited Work Based Learning

Chapter 11

Learning from the journey:
a triangulated approach

Veronica Swallow, Hazel Chalmers and John Miller

Introduction

In this book we have chosen to present a wide range of different perspectives relating to the development of AWBL. We have tried to capitalise upon the experiences that we have shared with our colleagues and students as we made the journey through the AWBL process during project based and programme based learning. Additionally, there has been an emphasis on the immense value of collaboration in creating such a responsive educational process; a process that ultimately leads to practitioner development via an extensive range of 'real world' practice developments.

According to Hargreaves (1994) collaborative cultures in education are usually spontaneous, voluntary, development orientated and unpredictable; in particular it is the outcomes that are often unpredictable because teachers in collaborative cultures can exercise some discretion over what is developed. Within the context of the drivers for change discussed by Professor Dunning in Chapter 2, the developments that have been outlined, explored and discussed in the remaining chapters are testimony to the collaborative culture in which AWBL has emerged; to the sometimes unpredictable nature of the AWBL process and the way in which the editors have at times needed to use discretion when developing the process.

Consequently the outcomes have sometimes been unpredictable but have been generally well received by students and employers (Swallow *et al.* 2000;

Chalmers, *et al.* 2001; Swallow *et al.* 2001). The spontaneity with which the different authors have responded to the challenges they encountered during the work based learning process has been alluded to many times throughout the book. Paralleling this has been an emphasis on the importance of ensuring that all Work Based Learning processes were subjected to the same degree of rigorous scrutiny and monitoring that other developments in Northumbria University and the NHS Trusts are exposed to.

In keeping with this philosophy, regular team meetings were held by the developers at which strategic and operational issues were discussed and an external examiner, was appointed who was informed about work based learning and sympathetic to the organic nature of the process of accreditation we were developing.

The moderation skills of the external examiner were such that:

- A value base of this kind of approach to learning and teaching was shared.
- All project based AWBL received both internal and external moderation giving greater confidence in quality assurance and consistency in standards.
- The development of 'standard' documents to explain and record processes leading to sharing of good practice.
- Advice and challenge made the teaching teams question and reflect upon their own approaches. Thus AWBL for providers became increasingly evidence based.
- Alternative solutions to concerns were offered by the external examiner which gave rise to learning for teachers.

Finally, we have endeavoured, where possible, to maximise our learning from the experience by reflecting upon and evaluating the AWBL process at different stages in order to inform our ongoing developments.

This spiralling process of Consultancy, Collaboration, Development, Implementation, Reflection, Evaluation and further Consultancy was necessary to allow the process to grow and mature and to allow the emergent issues to be uncovered and responded to. A more restrictive approach would have impeded the organic nature of AWBL. Hence what is described in this book is a dichotomous process that was at times, spontaneous, reactive and driven by the prevailing circumstances in health care and Higher Education (HE). At other times it was proactive and strategic, however, at all times it was purposefully driven by the need to provide a flexible, adaptable and rigorous mechanism for allowing practitioners' learning at work to be recognised, valued and accredited.

The need to reflect upon and evaluate educational interventions in health care has been alluded to in previous chapters; indeed the importance of reflection and evaluation is also well documented in published literature (Lincoln & Guba, 1986; Ovretveit, 1998) and policy (DoH, 1996; DoH, 1997; DoH, 1999; DoH, 2001).

Nevertheless, it is recognised that while there is always a will to carry out developmental evaluations in education it is often difficult to find sufficient resources to do so. The pace of change in health care and HE is so fast that competing demands for staff time and financial resources can inhibit developers who may wish to carry out evaluations simultaneous with new initiatives. No sooner is an initiative established then other opportunities present themselves which are equally interesting and demanding of time or resources. With the pace of change being so fast there is usually a drive to quickly respond to the needs of service developments and individual learner requirements. Hence the cycle of change often inhibits the desire to formally document the learning that has occurred in educational developments and sometimes, valuable information may be lost.

In this final chapter we consider the main factors which have influenced our practice in the ongoing development of AWBL and seek to capture the essence of the learning that has occurred for us since the first development. In the same way that the students' learning experiences have been responsive to service needs and individual learning needs, so too has our learning and that of our colleagues who were involved in commissioning the educational process central to the discussion in the book. In order to make the best use of our combined experiences and hopefully draw some meaningful conclusions which can help to inform the evidence base in this area we will draw upon a range of different sources of evidence. By taking this triangulated approach (Figure 1) we hope to maximise the learning inherent in the process and re-conceptualise the process of developing and delivering AWBL.

Figure I. A triangulated approach to evidence gathering.

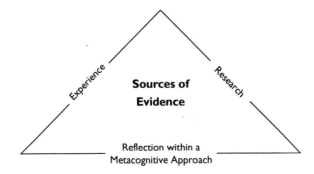

In the next part of this chapter, using a framework comprising the three sources of evidence outlined in Figure 1 we will discuss the learning that has taken place since the first AWBL development. Where appropriate we will use concepts and theories to help us to critically analyse the process that has informed the development of the Collaborative Dynamic Practitioner Development Model (CDPD Model).

Experience

In this first section we will, using the rich and varied discussion from the preceding chapters, summarise the experiences of students, service developers in health care and educationalists in relation to the development of AWBL. Experience as a source of learning and development has been widely discussed (Keeton & Tate, 1978; Kolb, 1984; Miles, 1987; Winter & Maisch, 1996) and the notions of informal and incidental learning are becoming well recognised in education (McGivney, 1999; Coffield, 2000; Eraut, 2000). The experiences recounted here are, therefore, valuable examples of work based learning for all the authors for whom much incidental and informal learning has occurred. Beckett (1999) suggests that life at work is typically experienced as an integration of feeling, thinking and doing where purposeful actions fill the day and workers interact with each other, deliberate over experiences and become increasingly aware of what is learned in the doing of the work, while the work is being undertaken. Typically, this awareness raising can take place incidentally or in a more formal way. When a worker is aware that they are learning from the experience then an organic learning phenomenon exists. The test of the experience having been learned from will be demonstrated by the contribution it makes to individual and perhaps organisational learning. To effectively promote workplace learning it is necessary for workers to exist in a culture that explicitly cultivates deliberate awareness of the learning as it occurs. Three simple prompts to provoke this work based learning response are proposed by Beckett and these are:

- What am I doing?
- Why am I doing it?
- What comes next?

In the accounts of many of the authors in this book there are examples, both implicit and explicit of these prompts having been used.

An example of this from the student perspective is in Chapter 7 where Julie Gillson and Mathew Brooksbank each recall the way they responded to their changing role while undertaking this new educational experience. Mathew's description of his difficulty in gaining the necessary opportunities to be supervised while practising new clinical skills show that after deliberation he took responsibility for negotiating new learning opportunities that would coincide with his changing shift patterns. Subsequently he,

> '... *learned more about the whole ethos of autonomy in this two week... could feel my confidence building. At last I felt comfortable with the thought of my new role.'* (Chapter 7)

Sarah Wimpenny (Chapter 8) describes the 'insider experience' of being responsible for organising 'in-house' training for qualified nursing staff in ITU during times of national bed shortages for patients needing intensive care. She describes how her own experiential learning while undertaking a course based AWBL process enabled her to recognise the potential in work based education for ITU staff. She gives several examples of work based educational material she has been involved in developing for use in critical care and advocates the role of clinical nurse educator to improve staffs' knowledge bases and subsequently their morale.

The value of learning by experience for service developers has been alluded to in particular in Chapters 4, 9 and 10. In Chapter 4, Chris Piercy and Bas Sen acknowledged that although the vision to develop major new role development for A&E nurses while ensuring they received appropriate education and academic recognition was clear, the method of implementation was not. Following the initial consultation process, early tensions arose between the stakeholders which led to a review of the strategy and development of a Project Management Group (PMG). This resulted in a much more focused, strategic and very successful approach to the development. In Chapter 9, Margaret Best describes the tripartite learning contract between herself, Jill Robson and John Miller as, '... *a forward looking alliance*' which quickly became a very important focus for managing the way in which they collectively considered the workplace learning. Margaret's discussion refers not only to Jill's learning as she was supported to implement 'Patient Focused Care' into a large NHS Trust but also how as they shared experiences and learned more they,

> '... *listened to and helped Jill as she addressed leadership issues and problems of change management. We watched as she found what worked and discussed why, and explored why the same approach could not be applied universally in all situations. We listened to her thoughts on leadership, what it was, how she led and where that matched what she was reading, why she disagreed in some instances. Together we explored past experiences – the hard job of learning to lead by example, having the confidence to let people free to make decisions and take appropriate actions. Developing staff who were nervous of decision-making roles (and then supporting or helping them before it got out of hand!).'*
> (Chapter 9)

In Chapter 10, Andrew Mellon, a Consultant Paediatrician who acted as Clinical Supervisor for Maggie Coates's Practice Project on the MA Advanced Practice suggests that the role of supervisor gradually develops and is influenced more by the various experiences and training opportunities that present themselves during a professional career. He goes on to say that many of the issues that arise in training for multi-professional roles are common to most adult learners. Therefore, both he and Maggie ask whether individual groups of health professionals working alongside each other can be encouraged to use the experience of shared learning to meet the ongoing demands of health care today.

The experience of educationalists has been explored and discussed in several chapters but in particular in Chapters 2, 3, 5 and 6. In Chapter 2, Professor Dunning discusses the changing contexts and trends she has experienced in HE and tells us that there is an increasing need for HE to be more accountable than in the past, accountable to its students and to society; the world of work has changed, the learners seeking education have changed and therefore, the status of practice based learning has changed.

In Chapter 3, Swallow, Chalmers and Miller explain that from Northumbria University's perspective AWBL combines the learning needs of different organisations and discuss the challenge faced by the University in developing the first AWBL Project for A&E nurses in Newcastle upon Tyne. An integration of Consultancy and Collaboration allowed the stakeholders from the Trust and Northumbria University to combine expertise to explore dilemmas and challenges and develop new possibilities to resolve them. However, as discussed by Piercy and Sen in Chapter 4, it was not until a partnership had been established through development of a PMT that the dilemmas and challenges were explored in a truly collaborative and egalitarian way and suitable resolutions were found.

The role of AWBL in developing Primary Health Care and Specialist Community Practice has been discussed in Chapters 5 and 6. In Chapter 5, John Unwin shares the experience of developing AWBL in Primary Health Care to meet the requirements of service developments and the need for an adequately trained workforce. Drawing on this experience he suggests that while AWBL can meet both these imperatives it can be a more costly alternative to traditional educational approaches. Therefore, he maintains that if organisations want the added [professional] value that AWBL has the potential to offer then they may find that a bespoke AWBL process will be more expensive than a traditional course.

In Chapter 6, Joanne Bennett describes the experience that she and a colleague underwent when using the AWBL framework to support community specialist practitioners in achieving degree/diploma level credit. In order to ensure the students' AWBL activity was relevant to practice a 'bottom-up' approach was used in developing the parameters of the project. Joanne describes how she and her colleague spent a great deal of time meeting with Trust based colleagues such as the Primary Care Manager and Clinical Leaders to learn from their experiences, and how collectively their confidence in this new process has increased through the mutual insight gained from these discussions.

In this section we have summarised some of the experiential learning that has occurred for the authors during their experience of AWBL and the evidence that has emerged from this. In the next section we will explore some of the evidence that has emerged from evaluation research conducted during and after specific AWBL activity already discussed in this book.

Research

In this section we use secondary data analysis (Sandelowski *et al.* 1997) from data pooled from three evaluation research studies relating to AWBL. The findings will be considered in relation to the theories and concepts discussed in earlier chapters. These evaluations are particularly relevant to the project based AWBL activity (referred to in Chapters 3, 4 and 7 which took place in the A&E Department, Newcastle upon Tyne) and the programme based AWBL activity (referred to in Chapter 8 as part of the BA [Hons] Nursing Practice) at Northumbria University. A summary of these evaluations is presented below:

- Evaluation of the development of the pilot project for AWBL in A&E.
- Evaluation of a development of a pilot for programme based AWBL (BA [Hons] Nursing Practice).
- The impact of AWBL on the developing role of the ENP (preliminary data analysis only available).

The aim of this analysis is to 'Determine the impact of Accredited Work Based Learning on practitioner development'.

Research design

As the views and experiences of professionals were the focus of the evaluations, qualitative methods were used (Strauss & Corbin, 1998; Murphy *et al.* 1998). The designs combined three different data sources (focus groups, collaborative learning groups and semi-structured interviews) involving a variety of different professionals. A developmental evaluation approach drawing on the social research tradition was adopted (Ovretveit, 1998). This approach contributes to changes in the development while the evaluation is being carried out and features include they:

- are local: for and with people in the development under evaluation.

- involve close collaboration: between the evaluator and provider at all stages of the evaluation.

- use continual feedback: applying emerging findings from the evaluation to the development during the evaluation process.

- usually consist of single or a few cases: the case being a service or organisation.

- use no controls: no attempt to control the evaluated or create experimental and control groups.

- are a non-experimental design.

- are inductive: concepts and theories are often built up inductively out of the data gathered.

- usually involve qualitative methods (adapted from Ovretveit, 1998).

Ethical considerations

The evaluations were conducted in accordance with Northumbria University's ethical requirements for research and evaluation studies. Written consent was obtained from all participants and anonymity of the data source was maintained. All information obtained during the studies was used to inform an understanding of the processes and was stored securely when not in use. All tape recordings are being erased after completion of the evaluation and dissemination of findings is complete.

Data analysis

All data were analysed using the Framework Technique (Ritchie & Spencer, 1994; Swallow *et al.* 2002). This method is systematic, thorough and grounded in the data but also flexible and enables easy retrieval of data to show others. In addition it allows both between and within case analysis and involves a process of: familiarisation with the data; identification of recurrent themes; indexing; charting; abstraction and interpretation. The data was viewed separately by two members of educational/research staff and validation of findings was achieved through comparative exploration of the outcomes of the process. In this way, topics and themes within each data source were identified. Establishing the credibility of qualitative research increases the likelihood that findings will be applied to practice (Lincoln & Guba, 1986) and according to Maykut and Morehouse (1994) the ultimate test of trustworthiness is whether we believe the findings strongly enough to act on them.

Findings

Studies 1 and 2 were both designed to evaluate the development of AWBL while Study 3 was designed to evaluate the impact of AWBL on ENP role development. An aggregate of primary and secondary data analysis from the three studies uncovered three main themes relating to the issue of practitioner development as it is influenced by the AWBL approach.

These themes are:

- Professional competence
- Personal confidence
- Learning cultures.

They will be discussed in more detail below.

Professional competence

The practitioners involved in both project based and course based AWBL developments agreed that it provided recognition of skills development [practical and academic] through accreditation and although it was hard work and more time consuming than some had anticipated, the fact that it was available for different levels of learning increased its adaptability for the learner (Swallow *et al.* 2001). The ENPs, however, in discussing their developing professional competence as they adapted to their new roles described how initially they felt exposed to criticism from nursing and medical peers as they needed to practice new clinical skills and demonstrate an increased knowledge base to underpin the new skills (Swallow *et al.* 2000). However, in the collaborative learning groups ENPs began to explore the way they had become aware of the advantages of reflection as a means of learning how to handle these fears.

> *'It [reflection] was new, unique... I'd probably never heard of reflection... now by reflecting on the learning we can articulate with them [medical colleagues] on their level.'*

All ENPs described going through a period of feeling de-skilled, before developing this new confidence in their own competence and anticipated that their new role had potential to improve the service for patients by reducing waiting time but also because they,:

> *'... provide a more holistic package of care because we look after all aspects of the patients problems – not just the injury but its possible impact on their life.'*

All participants identified issues of infrastructure and changing professional boundaries as central to the process of implementing the project based AWBL.

Building on this background the role has now evolved in response to the ongoing service developments.

Personal confidence

The need to develop personal learning outcomes at the start of the course based AWBL was a new and challenging experience that was initially difficult but because,

> '... it was an individual learning pathway rather than a generic pathway we all did it slightly differently, that is probably what is so good about it.'
> (AWBL Student BA [Hons] Nursing Practice)

The synergy between clinical and academic development led to rapid learning and any initial scepticism about the flexible nature of the process was overcome by a positive impact on personal and professional self-confidence arising from peer recognition of practice developments linked to the achievement of personal learning outcomes.

ENPs have become more assertive and empowered by critical/reflective skills enhanced during AWBL as is evidenced by the following quote made during the final collaborative learning group.

> 'Protocols don't now give any scope for clinical judgement... we need to be able to write them ourselves.' (ENP)

This increasing confidence displayed by the ENPs as they are taking responsibility for beginning to define the future direction of their role is entirely consistent with Eraut's (1994) definition of competence which he claims is an integration of capability and performance which results in a critical and flexible approach to practice that enables a person to become a proponent of change and creator of new professional knowledge. In discussing the fact that ENPs now independently manage entire caseloads of patients presenting with minor injuries an ENP made the following observation,

> '... they [Drs] are having to release some of that power that used to be all theirs.'
> (ENP)

Learning cultures

At the outset of the project development, the broad expectation associated with the culture into which the AWBL was introduced was that roles and responsibilities for planning and delivery would naturally evolve, however, it quickly became evident that the entire project would need some strategic direction in order to meet its objectives and make most effective use of the resources.

'I think from the outset we should have had a Project Management Team and we didn't... we learnt from it and developed a PMT.' (Head of Nursing)

As outlined in Chapter 1, many professionals who undertake learning at work are already members of the workplace culture and have developed their own strategies for managing uncertainty and new situations, however, they may be novices in making explicit the implicit knowledge they use daily and the sources of that knowledge (Lave & Wenger, 1991; Cope *et al.* 2000). These learners may already have personal constructs of professional practice derived from their social context and culture so their learning is best focused on questioning those constructs and engaging with the change process. This involves accepting that there is more than one 'right' answer, dealing with uncertainty and the capacity to use existing competence in unfamiliar contexts by extending and adapting existing skills.

Guided discussion during the collaborative learning groups with ENPs found that those who were more experienced as they had been part of the first cohort to take part in the AWBL project saw it as a means of education and training that provided relevant, responsive and flexible learning in a dynamic health care setting. In addition it enabled them to articulate the issues that were important to them in relation to their clinical and academic development. During the group discussion it also became evident that the experienced ENPs were acting as mentors and facilitators of learning for the newly appointed ENPs. In turn the new ENPs described themselves as novices and,

'... we (new ENPs) look to you (experienced ENPs) for guidance and advice on the new clinical skills but also the way to handle things with Drs and that...'

This resulting socialiasation of new ENPs into 'communal enterprise' was described by Cope *et al.* (2000) as cognitive apprenticeship in which the 'expert' was making explicit the strategies by which the 'novice' could develop competence.

There was also evidence from ENPs and other professionals who were involved in semi-structured interviews to explore the impact of AWBL on the emerging role of the ENP that there was increasing multidisciplinary acceptance of the new ENP role. This manifested itself in several ways and the following comments are examples of this.

'Medical schools are not preparing doctors in communicating with patients properly and that is something we have learnt from ENPs and other nurses.' (Consultant A&E)

'Working to protocols for a few months, a year – but after that they (ENPs) must be given freedom to develop their own practice.' (Consultant)

In this section we have briefly summarised some of the research evidence that has emerged since the developments began.

Reflection within a metacognitive approach

In this final section and in keeping with the philosophy of AWBL we will ourselves reflect upon the learning that has occurred during the process of developing AWBL and compiling this book with our colleagues and students. This third source of evidence will help us to synthesise our learning. To support our reflections we will use an adaptation of a metacognitive model (Figure 2) that operationalises the process of reflection. This model is particularly pertinent as it was developed in an HE setting by McAlpine *et al.* (1999) who undertook a programme of research to document the way experienced teachers in HE go about their day-to-day business of planning, instructing and evaluating learners.

The model proposed by McAlpine *et al.* (1999) is conceived to have six components: goals; knowledge; action; monitoring; decision-making and corridor of tolerance. For the purpose of this analysis we will use the first five components. It represents an iterative process involving both thought and action and according to Yinger (1990) can be regarded as an ongoing conversation between present action, past experience and future intentions. The model is explanatory rather than predictive. A brief explanation of the model follows.

Reflection is visualised within this model as continuous interaction between the components of action and knowledge. *Action* represents the external arena in

Figure 2. Metacognitive model (adapted from McAlpine *et al.*, 1999).

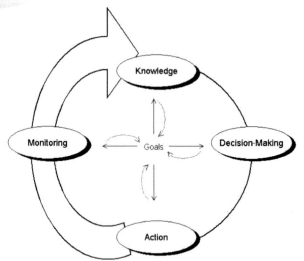

which plans are enacted, cognitions are transformed into behaviours and goals implemented. Knowledge represents in-depth cognitive structures accumulated through a combination of training and experience. 'Content knowledge' refers to the subject matter of teaching while 'general pedagogical knowledge' refers to general principles and strategies of teaching that transcend subject matter. 'Pedagogical' content knowledge refers to the way subjects are formulated to make them comprehensible to learners. 'Knowledge of learners' includes knowledge of the characteristics that different students bring to the situation. Yet another perspective on knowledge is the teacher's development of professional knowledge through experience and finally that of the teacher's tacit knowledge. Thus knowledge can be used in the creation of plans that provide a mechanism for monitoring and decision-making that make up the process of reflection and it is these plans that enable the meeting of goals.

The concept of goals highlights directed behaviour as central to the model because although goals usually remain relatively constant they both constrain and direct the other features of the model and feedback from the other components may lead to a change in the goals. The model sees the concepts of monitoring and decision-making as mechanisms that link knowledge and action but which are also directed and constrained by goals. Monitoring of clues in the external environment provides feedback about what is happening during enactment.

With this model in mind, we will briefly reflect upon the learning that has occurred for us during the AWBL process.

Reflections on our experience

Action and knowledge

With regard to the experience of developing AWBL within this concept we see reflection as a continuous interaction between action and knowledge. Thus through the ongoing process of consultancy, collaboration, development and implementation we saw the plans we had made being put into action and where necessary made adjustments to our teaching. In this process we drew upon the knowledge that we each already possessed and as we moved through the process we saw the collaborative partnership move from a position of information exchange to one where we jointly generated possible solutions. Thus the collaborative relationship kept shifting and changing as goals were redefined in response to the specific circumstances.

The facilitative approach we adopted to teaching enabled us to draw upon the students' specialised knowledge and experience and through a tripartite learning contract they were supported to develop individual learning outcomes relating to service needs, personal areas of interest and identified learning needs. In this way we used the 'knowledge of the learners' acquired when they completed a personal profiling exercise at the beginning of the AWBL process to help us draw on the domain of 'general pedagogical knowledge' to help make the particular subject areas they had identified, comprehensible to them.

Goals represents our collective expectations of what was to be accomplished and provided the basis for what actions we should take to achieve them. Our goals fell into two categories; those focusing on teaching which were to some extent under our control, and those focusing on students' learning which were not necessarily under our control. In the first category, we set initial goals during the consultancy relating to the development of the collaborative partnership and later the methods of teaching that would help in achievement of these goals. As discussed previously (Chalmers *et al.* 2001) it became necessary on occasions to adjust goals in order, for instance, to ensure the ENPs received appropriate clinical shadowing from A&E Consultants in the workplace to allow them to practice and achieve the pre-determined clinical competencies.

In the second category, it was necessary for us to sometimes adopt novel teaching and learning strategies such as work based seminars/tutorials that often needed to be rescheduled or take place in a fragmented way in a busy A&E department. Although this facilitative teaching approach was still goal directed, i.e. intended to enable practitioners to achieve their individual learning outcomes, our achievement of these goals was sometimes outside our control and required us to take a very flexible and adaptable approach.

Monitoring is the mechanism by which the relation between intended plans and actual actions is tracked (McAlpine *et al.* 1999). A particular issue that we monitored was the delay in having agreement of the input from professional colleagues who would facilitate some of the clinical skills development of the nurses. There were issues relating to their time and reimbursement which delayed the beginning of the seminars. Thus decision-making led to establishment of an infrastructure to manage the implementation of the education, to create the necessary learning environment and to support the nurses in their learning and ultimately in their new roles.

A great deal of 'post hoc' learning took place for us. As well as reflecting upon and deliberating over issues as and when they arose, we have gained a great deal of post hoc understanding in the process of editing this book, both by discussing with our colleagues and students their contributions and while reading and reviewing their finished contributions. This, therefore, confirms our view that the spiral of learning in the CDPD Model (Figure 3) is continually evolving and will continue to do so and this illustrates how flexible the model is and how adaptable it could be for use in today's changing world of health care.

Figure 3. Collaborative Dynamic Practitioner Development Model
(CDPD Model)

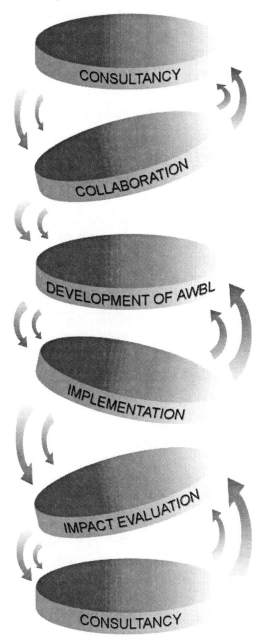

References

Beckett, D. (1999) *Past the guru and up the garden path: the new organic management learning* in Boud, D. and Garrick, J. (eds) *Understanding Learning at Work* (Routledge, London).

Chalmers, H., Swallow, V. and Miller, J. (2001) 'Accredited Work Based Learning: an approach for collaboration between Higher Education and practice.' *Nurse Education Today* pp. 21, 587–606.

Coffield, F. (2000) *The necessity of informal learning* (The Policy Press, Bristol).

Cope, P., Cuthbertson, P. and Stoddart, B. (2000) 'Situated learning in the practice placement,' *Journal of Advanced Nursing* 31 (4) pp. 850–856.

Department of Health (1997) *The New NHS: Modern and Dependable* (HMSO, London).

Department of Health (1999) *Making a Difference: Strengthening the Nursing, Midwifery and Health Visiting Contribution to Health and Health Care* (HMSO, London)

Eraut, M. (1994) *Developing Professional Knowledge and Competence* (The Falmer Press, London).

Eraut, M. (2000) *Non-formal learning, implicit learning and tacit knowledge in professional work*, in F. Coffield (ed.) *The necessity of informal learning* (The Policy Press, Bristol).

Hargreaves, A. (1994) *Changing teachers: changing times* (Cassell, London).

Keeton, M. and Tate, P. (1978) *Learning by experience – What, Why, How.* (Jossey-Bass, San Francisco).

Kolb, D.A. (1984) *Experiential Learning: Experience as the source of learning and development* (Prentice-Hall, Inc. New Jersey).

Lave, J. and Wenger, E. (1991) *Situated Learning: Legitimate peripheral participation* (Cambridge University Press, Cambridge).

Lincoln, Y.S. and Guba, E.G. (1986) 'Research, evaluation and policy analysis; heuristics for disciplined enquiry'. *Policy Studies Review*, 5, pp. 546–565.

McAlpine, L., Weston, C., Beauchamp, J., Wiseman, C. and Beauchamp, C. (1999) 'Building a metacognitive model of reflection.' *Higher Education* (37) pp. 105–131.

McGivney, V. (1999) *Informal learning in the community: a trigger for change and development* (National Institute of Adult Continuing Education [NIACE], Leicester).

Miles, R. (1987) '*Experiential Learning in the Curriculum*' in the *Curriculum in Nurse Education*, P. Allen and M. Jolley (eds). (Croom Helm, New York) pp. 85–125.

Murphy, E., Dingwell, R. and Greatbatch, D. *et al.* (1998) *Qualitative research methods in HTA: a review of the literature* (HTA Southampton) 2 (16).

Ovretveit, J. (1998) *Evaluating Health Interventions: an introduction to evaluation of health treatments, services, policies and organisational interventions* (Open University Press, Buckingham).

Ritchie, J. and Spencer, L. (1994) *Qualitative data analysis for applied policy research* in *Analysing Qualitative Data* Bryman, A. and Burgess, R. (eds) (Routledge, London) pp. 173–194.

Sandelowski, M., Dicherty, S. and Emden, C. (1997) 'Qualitative metasynthesis: Issues and techniques.' *Research in Nursing and Health* (20) pp. 365–371.

Strauss, A. and Corbin, J. (1998) *Basic of qualitative research*. (Sage, CA).

Swallow, V., Chalmers, H., Miller, J., Piercy, C., Sen, B. and Gibb, C. (2000) 'Evaluating the development of an Accredited Work Based Learning (AWBL) scheme for A&E nurses.' *Emergency Nurse* 8(7) pp. 33–39.

Swallow, V., Chalmers, H. and Miller, J. (2001) 'Accredited Work Based Learning (AWBL) for new nursing roles: nurses' experiences of two pilot schemes.' *Journal of Clinical Nursing – Research in Brief* (10) pp. 820–821.

Swallow, V., Newton, J. and van Lottom, C. (2002) 'How to manage and display qualitative data using Framework and Microsoft Excel.' *Journal of Clinical Nursing* (in press).

Winter, R. and Maisch, M. (1996) *Professional Competence and Higher Education: The ASSET Programme* (The Falmer Press, London).

Yinger, R. (1990) *The conversation of practice* in Clift, R.T., Houston, W.R. and Pugach, M.C. (eds) *Encouraging Reflective Practice in Education* (Teachers College Press, New York) pp. 72–96.

Appendix

Clinical skills training

As part of the MA programme, nurses in adult practice undertook a module aimed at increasing their skills in recognising acute potentially serious problems. This required a more medically based systems approach to clinical assessment than was used in everyday nursing practice. The adult nature of this module did not seem appropriate to a paediatric trained nurse and it was agreed that this part of the programme would be better delivered in a paediatric setting. The aim was to transpose this into the context of a community children's nurse working independently in the community and to use a system for clinical assessment that would aid identification of sick children who might require acute medical interventions in addition to their expected nursing care.

In undertaking training with a medical assessment model it was important that this would be recognised by other members of the acute paediatric team, as well as by other nursing staff. The most appropriate way to structure the training was by using the model for assessment of sick children that is the backbone of Advanced Paediatric Life Support (APLS) training. This is used increasingly in a multi-professional way throughout paediatric departments in the UK. All junior doctors undergo a one-day training course and the majority of middle grade and senior staff undertake a three-day training course using these principles. It is also becoming common for members of paediatric nursing teams in a variety of settings to undertake these courses and be familiar with their concepts. APLS training has a number of key components, which seemed to lend themselves to use in this module:

1. Providing skills to assess and manage critically ill children in the first hour of admission to hospital. However, a major thrust of the APLS training is to recognise ill children before they deteriorate and expedite care.

2. Recognition of the sick child – looks at features of illness and how they may lead through a common pathway of respiratory failure, circulatory failure and central neurological failure to cardio-respiratory arrest. The aim is to give a common language to those caring for sick children to be able to give specific reasons why they recognise that a child is sick and hence to aid communication at a distance, increase overt recognition of signs of serious illness and hopefully reduce risk to the sick child by ensuring timely interventions.

3. Individual systems assessment and more detailed assessment of clinical problems:
   • Respiratory problems
   • Shock
   • Collapse.

The guide for the module was the Advanced Paediatric Life Support (APLS) Manual, using relevant chapters to address these areas of study. Tutorials were held with the clinical supervisor at which the content of the chapters was discussed and practical teaching of necessary clinical skills undertaken. Supervision of this module was aided by previous experience of the supervisor as an APLS instructor, which involved successful completion of a three-day APLS course, completion of a generic 3-day life support instructor training course and attendance at two APLS courses per year as an instructor to develop and maintain instructor status. Assessment through the clinical skills module was undertaken in part by formative ongoing assessment of progress during tutorials, but a final summative assessment based on the same model as the adult practitioners was undertaken. This was in the setting of a semi-structured observational examination, relying on observation and identification of key components of the taught approach in assessing children in a ward setting using the structured approach to recognition of the seriously ill child in their assessment.

Contributor's profiles

Joanne Bennett
MA Social Policy, BA Psychology/Sociology, RN, NDN, RNT

Joanne is a Principal Lecturer at Northumbria University. Her current post is in Primary Care Development within the School of Health, Community and Education Studies. She has a clinical background in community nursing and has been in education for 15 years.

Margaret Best
RN, RM, ONC Dip in Nursing (Lon) with distinction, NCSS

Margaret is recently retired as Director of Nursing and Quality from North Durham Health Care NHS Trust. Clinical background in Trauma and Orthopaedics. She has been a Director of Nursing for 22 years in different NHS locations. Specialist areas: Involving the public in full participation of NHS Development, Development of Ward Sisters, Complaints and Quality of Nursing and Clinical Care.

Mathew Brooksbank
RGN, Dip He (Child), BSc (Nursing), MA Advanced Practice (Nursing)

Currently works as a Primary and Emergency Nurse Practitioner, Newcastle Hospitals NHS Trust.

Hazel Chalmers
MPhil, MA (Education), RGN, DN, RNT

Hazel is a Principal Lecturer in Northumbria University. Her current post is Learning and Teaching Support within the School of Health, Community and Education Studies. She has a clinical background of community nursing and has been in Higher Education for over 20 years. Her areas of research and interest are curriculum development and quality assurance.

Maggie Coates
MA Advanced Practice (Nursing) RGN, RSCN, HV

A Senior Lecturer at Northumbria University Maggie's current post is within the School of Health, Community and Education Studies. She has a clinical background of paediatrics within both acute and community nursing.

Mary Dunning
MA Curriculum Studies, RNT, RM, RGN

Mary is a Professor and Deputy Dean of the School of Health, Community and Education Studies at Northumbria University. Her current role involves academic development and quality assurance both for the School and the University. Having worked in general nursing as a Ward Sister she moved into nurse education over 20 years ago, becoming the Principal of Bede, Newcastle and Northumbria College of Health Studies. She moved with the College into Higher Education in 1995. Nationally she was Chairperson of the National Directors of Nurse Education Group and a member of the Chief Nurse's Advisory Education Group for England. Her particular areas of interest are in quality assurance, widening access and participation into Higher Education programmes, curriculum innovation and evaluation for the health and social care professions.

Patrick Easen
PhD, BEd, FRSA

Patrick is a Professor and Associate Dean of the School of Health, Community and Education Studies at Northumbria University. His current role involves looking after the University's provision for intending and serving teachers and linked professionals. Previously he has worked at both the University of Newcastle upon Tyne and the Open University. He has also been a primary teacher in several schools. He has produced a number of publications on practice development.

Julie Gillson
RGN, Dip. Management, Dip. HE (Child) Honorary Research Associate

Julie's current post is Paediatric and Adult Emergency Nurse Practitioner, Newcastle upon Tyne Hospitals NHS Trust. She is taking an active part in the Modernisation Agency's Emergency Services Collaboration and has a growing interest in increasing nursing research capacity within the Accident and Emergency department.

Andrew Mellon
BSc, MB, BS, FRCPCH, Cert Med Ed (Newcastle)

A Consultant Paediatrician in the department of paediatrics at Sunderland Royal Hospital and honorary lecturer in Child Health at the University of Newcastle upon Tyne. His current post is divided between paediatrics and undergraduate medical education in Sunderland, as well as being a tutor on 'Diploma of Medical Education' course at Newcastle and Regional Adviser for training in paediatrics in the Northern Region of the NHS in England. He has been involved in educational supervision at both undergraduate and postgraduate level in medicine, and across professional boundaries since his appointment in 1996. His areas of interest include assessment, self-directed learning and professional development.

John Miller
MSc, BSc (Hons), RGN, RMN, RNT, DN

John is the Associate Dean, Business and International Development, within the School of Health, Community and Education Studies. Having worked in both general and mental health nursing environments, he moved into nurse education, before taking up a post in Higher Education almost 15 years ago. His research interests revolve around practice and practitioner development.

Chris Piercy
BSc (Hons), RGN, RMN, Dip HSM, FEATC, MBA

Chris is the Director of Nursing and Community Services for Gateshead Primary Care Trust, a post held since 1 November 2002. Prior to this Chris spent 30 years in Acute Adult nursing and mental health in a variety of organisations. He is particularly interested in multi-professional practice development and developing new roles for nurses and AHPs. He is keen to expand the research capacity of front-line nurses and AHP's.

Jill Robson
MA, BSc Dip RGN

Jill is a modern matron at the University Hospital of Durham. Her current area of responsibility includes plastic surgery and a multi-speciality unit. She has 25 years of nursing experience including clinical teacher, ward sister, and senior sister posts. Her areas of practice development include Patient Focus Care, including multidisciplinary pathways of care, multi-skilling and wound care.

Bas Sen
MBBS, FRCS, FFAEM

Bas is a Consultant, Clinical Lecturer and Head of the A&E Department, Newcastle General hospital. He has been a Consultant since 1993 and his interests lie in exploring innovative ways of providing quality service in the NHS. Nationally he has held posts with working parties in The Resuscitation Council UK and is currently involved with the NHS Modernisation Agency as the Trust's Clinical Lead for the Emergency Service's Collaborative to explore more effective ways of working and implementing change.

Veronica Swallow
MMedSci, BSc (Hons), RGN, RSCN, PCAP

Veronica is a Senior Lecturer, Division of Learning in Organisations, School of Health, Community and Education Studies at Northumbria University. She has a clinical background in adult and paediatric nursing and has worked in Higher Education for four years. Her particular areas of interest in education and research include learning and competence development of health care users and practitioners.

Sarah Wimpenny
RGN, BA (Hons) in Nursing Practice

A G grade Sister in Critical Care Royal Victoria Infirmary, Newcastle upon Tyne, Sarah has 10 years critical care experience and a particular interest in nurse education and development.

List of acronyms

A&E – Accident and Emergency

ASR – Acute Services Review

AWBL – Accredited Work Based Learning

CPD – Continuing Professional Development

ENP – Emergency Nurse Practitioner

HE – Higher Education

HEFCE – Higher Education Funding Council England

HEI – Higher Education Institution

LEO – Leading an Empowered Organisation

MIU – Minor Injuries Unit

NHS – National Health Service

OSCE – Objective Structured Clinical Examination

PMG – Programme Management Group

RGN – Registered General Nurse

RSCN – Registered Sick Children's Nurse

SHO – Senior House Officer

WIC – Walk-in Centre